WHAT EVERY WOMAN SHOULD KNOW
ABOUT HER HUSBAND'S MONEY

What Every Woman Should Know About Her Husband's Money

Shelby White

Random House
New York

This work was published in hardcover and in different form
by Turtle Bay Books, a division of Random House, Inc.,
New York, in 1992.

Library of Congress Cataloging-in-Publication Data

White, Shelby.
    What every woman should know about her husband's
money / Shelby White
    Includes bibliographical references and index.
        p. cm.
    ISBN 0-679-75816-X
    1. Married women—Finance, Personal. I. Title.
HG179.W524 1995
332.024' 0655—dc20   94-45441

Manufactured in the United States of America on
acid-free paper
98765432
First Paperback Edition

To my mother and father who, after sixty years of marriage, still share everything. And, of course, to Leon and Tracy.

Contents

WHAT EVERY WOMAN SHOULD KNOW
ABOUT HER HUSBAND'S MONEY

1.
Marriage Is Not an Equal Opportunity

When Barbara Walters signed her first million-dollar television contract, she reportedly said to her agent, "Promise me that in five years I won't have to marry for money." Curious about this comment, I once asked her if she had been quoted accurately. "Yes," she said, and then explained that, although she knew how to earn money, she didn't know how to manage it. She had accumulated some money and then turned it over to a friend, a highly regarded Wall Street expert, to invest for her. The results were disastrous. She lost a substantial amount and worried that it could happen again.

Barbara Walters, like many women, reflected the view that money was a man's domain and, in the end, a man will rescue a woman from financial woes. Barbara Walters also found out that this is not necessarily true. Yet many women, whether based on a tradition of dependence or the reality of lower wages, have a fear of financial ruin. Even women with substantial earnings power report "bag lady nightmare"—a feeling described as "a pervasive uneasiness that despite all their affluence and hard work they will end up destitute."[1]

When it comes to money and marriage, old stereotypes persist. Women have been coming out of the kitchen and going off to work for the past twenty-five years. We have had a sexual revolution, a divorce revolution, and a work revolution. The marriage revolution is not here yet. We have entered into an era of gender-neutral language that has attempted to eliminate the sexism in our vocabularies. Our legal system purports not to distinguish between males and females; our classrooms are enrolling more women than ever in areas previously reserved for males.[2]

Despite these changes, the promised equality has not materialized. Inside the home tradition takes root. We may have blended families and extended families, but we still have families. And in the privacy of our families, women are not equal. Women still take care of the inside of the house, pay the daily bills, and take care of the children. Their husbands do the outdoor work and manage the assets.[3] Men and women continue to define their roles in marriage according to traditional tasks. Men think of themselves as the breadwinners.[4] For men, the leading definition of masculinity is being "a good provider for his family." Men equate money with power and self-esteem, and women agree. Women think of men who earn a lot of money as masculine and powerful. In contrast, women think the definition of femininity is being able to balance work and home and to care for people. Men think femininity is defined as sexual attraction.[5]

This homage to tradition persists despite the overwhelming number of two-income couples.[6] Over 31 million married women are helping to bring home the money. In three quarters of the families with incomes above $125,000, the high earnings are a result of joint efforts.[7]

For generations American marriages were bound by a legal system that gave power to husbands. Now, the laws have changed. Modern marriage is supposed to be about equals. The problem is, men are resisting the change and continuing to use their higher earnings as a way to control their marriages. Women have adapted to working outside the home, but men have not as easily adapted to having working wives. Men are still reluctant to share the housekeeping. The more money a husband earns, the less willing he is to do the housework, no matter how many hours his wife works outside the home.[8] When children come along, the traditional roles are further entrenched.

What is control? How does it work in marriage? It means that a husband can make decisions to which his wife is afraid to object. As one woman said, "I was always afraid I would find myself out on the street with three children." She didn't feel she had any rights because she didn't earn the money.

Sometimes control is subtle. One example is the two-paycheck couple that argues about which one of them will pick up the children at school. The one with the lower paycheck usually picks up the children. The argument appears to be about time and responsibility, but it is really about power and control.

Sometimes the control is more direct. A typical example would be the husband who decides to buy an expensive stereo set even though his wife would prefer that the money be spent on clothes for the children. He earns the money so he gets to buy the stereo. It is not surprising to discover that the more money the man earns, the more likely that he will manage the assets.[9] The only leverage she has, said one wife, is to withhold sex.

For many women brought up to think they would be

equal financial partners in marriage, reality comes as an unpleasant surprise. Frequently there is a big change from when the couple dated and each paid their own way. When they married they probably continued to split expenses. For many women, the arrival of children means a dramatic shift in the balance of their marriages. For one thing, the husband may suddenly see his wife as a mother and want her to assume a more traditional role. Then too, a wife may discover that she can no longer keep up her end financially. This is especially true if she stops working, a decision both make together, but which has a much greater impact on the wife.

The equality women thought they would have at work hasn't really happened either. Women as a group are paid less than men. Notice, I said paid. Usually headlines read, women continue to "earn" less than men, making it seem as if women were somehow less deserving than men. In general women are paid 71 percent of what men are paid. Executive women do only 57 percent as well as executive men. The statistics vary, but rarely do women do better than men.[10] Women are more apt to interrupt their careers to raise their children. When they do, they are likely to fall behind men in the wage race. Women who go back to work after they have taken time off may have to accept a lower paying job, or they may lose some pension benefits or seniority at their former jobs. And this fourteen years after the Pregnancy Discrimination Act was passed, which was supposed to protect women.

Many women take less demanding jobs in order to spend more time home with their children. Many women graduating from law school take jobs in legal departments of large corporations, instead of trying for more lucrative law firm partnerships. And guess what? Women who work as lawyers for large corporations are paid less than male lawyers in similar jobs.[11]

Women who enter fields formerly reserved for men also find resegregation, with women getting the caretaker jobs: more women doctors become pediatricians, the lowest paid field, than brain surgeons, one of the highest paid areas of medicine.

A growing number of women are discovering that they also must take care of their elderly parents, and their husband's elderly parents, as well. In February 1990, when Annalyn Swan, formerly editor of *Savvy* magazine, announced that she would leave her job, she told her readers, "Life has a way of making certain decisions for you. In my case it was the illness of a parent. Faced with the prospect of frequent travel and intensive care, I realized, like many other women, just how much our society still depends for caregiving on women. For me, at least, the choice was clear. Life became a matter of being not just an editor but, more importantly, a daughter." Swan is "sequencing," the term sociologists apply to the trading of office jobs for more independent projects. Swan writes that more women will opt to do this. Imagine reading a "swan song" like hers from a male editor in chief.

The income women have been bringing home has been a mixed blessing. Some men like it, but many men feel threatened when their wives work and become more independent.[12] And no wonder. Men have a lot to lose. When a wife works, she not only brings home a paycheck, but she also continues to do most of the housework and takes care of the kids. Not a bad deal for her husband. She also begins to have a separate life. Older husbands resent wives who usurp their traditional role. Perhaps this is because many women work because their husbands do not earn enough. The husband already feels inadequate, since he is not fulfilling his expected role of supporting his family. Many women, capable of earning even more than their husbands, sense their husbands' discomfort. They decide they would rather have the marriage than the career, so they pull back.

Of course, husbands outearn their wives in almost 80 percent of families. Therefore, the wife's work is deemed less important and less essential. His salary is considered crucial, hers incidental. This frequently turns into the "I can't afford to work" syndrome. This means, after baby-sitters, transportation, clothing, and taxes are deducted from the wife's salary, the additional income is too small to warrant the time and effort. Many couples discover that up to two thirds of the second paycheck goes to child care, household help, clothing, food, and work-related expenses. The result—the wife stays home. The husband seldom gives up his job, because he is usually earning more money. Nor is the child-care cost considered as coming from the husband's salary.[13] Little economic value is given to the wife's unpaid household work of running the house, managing the children, or arranging the social schedule.

In lower income, younger families, when wives discover they are capable of earning a living—and maybe earning more than their husbands—it is the wife who becomes dissatisfied and often wants to leave the marriage.[14] Although there have been studies showing women plunging into poverty immediately after divorce, many women, liberated from the constraints of marriage, actually work harder and earn more than women who remain married. The marriage itself may be a reason women earn less money.

Sociologists, not surprisingly, have begun to discover a high correlation between women going to work and the divorce rate in America.[15]

Working part-time is not much of an improvement. June Ryan is typical.* Trained as a biologist, when I met her she was seven months pregnant. She and her husband bought a small house in the suburbs. June became a laboratory technician so that she could plan a work schedule that would allow her to be at home most of the time. In the three years since their daughter was born, June has continued to work at a job that pays her only an hourly wage with no benefits. Her husband Bill's career at a large corporation has continued to advance.

Although she was once able to support herself, the arrival of a baby and the overhead of a house have added expenses that June could no longer manage on her own. She has become financially dependent. Her lower earnings have put her in a position in which her husband can use his higher wages as a reason to handle the assets and otherwise control the finances of their marriage.

Many women, frustrated by a glass ceiling at the office, stay home and become just as dependent on their husbands as the mothers they had vowed not to imitate once did.

Only with a difference. Their mothers expected to stay home. In the nineties, women feel dependent, but they also feel guilty if they stay home with their children. On

---

*Not a real name. Throughout the book I have used fictitious names.

the other hand, women who try both to work and to raise children are often too frazzled to do either job well. A wife finds herself with two careers: working mother and working woman. Her husband has only his career.

The wife who earns less or who has stayed home to take care of the children feels that she is not entitled to a say in the finances. One woman, now home caring for children, confided that her husband, sensing her unhappiness at feeling dependent, put money into her savings account every month. She only resented his attempt to "pay" her.

Today many women are saying no to this paternalism. While it is easier for the working woman to do this, because she has some economic leverage, the woman who stays home and cares for the children and helps her husband by entertaining his clients and otherwise freeing him from household chores to be able to devote himself to business, also has a right to share in the finances of the marriage, as partner and decision maker.

Obviously, there are some marriages that thrive on the powerful-husband/weak-and-protected-wife relationship. One woman said, "I always saw my husband as the merchant prince, and he always saw me as the student." When her husband had business losses neither one of them could discuss it because it would have destroyed the myths each had created about the other.

When people marry they bring their own attitudes about money with them. These attitudes tend to color the way they handle money in their marriages. The wife who was brought up in a home where her parents both worked and kept their money separate may feel guilty if her husband pays for her. The wife who was brought up in a more traditional household may feel uncomfortable if her husband doesn't pay for her. The woman who equates money with love may be disappointed if her husband doesn't buy her expensive presents.

Patterns of spending are also usually carried over from our own childhood. The wife who was brought up by thrifty parents hates to spend money unless she gets good value. The wife who hated eating in expensive restaurants ruined such occasions for her husband because she always looked at the prices and then calculated the cost of the ingredients.

The husband who saw his mother struggle after his father died and left the family with little money wants to put all his money into insurance. If he is married to a woman whose family never believed in worrying about that rainy day, conflicts can result.

Unfortunately, many couples who are easily able to discuss sex with each other enter marriage without ever discussing just how they will manage their finances.

Money conflicts are different from control. You may want to save every penny for a house in five years, while your husband may want to spend more now and buy a less expensive house. You may want to invest in a new business; your husband may want to support his ailing mother. You may not mind owing money; your husband may hate it. These are legitimate conflicts open to discussion and compromise. And, let's face it, some pretty tense arguments. Control in the marriage is different. It means you may be forced to do things without discussion, without even knowing the facts.

Today, no woman should be ignorant of her husband's finances or her own. If a wife doesn't share financial decisions, regardless of who earns the money, her husband will act as the powerful daddy. By having to ask, you give up control and then money is used as a reward. Do what your husband would like and he will get you the car you want.

If your husband is reading this book he may be saying to himself, "I try and tell her, but every time I start to talk about taxes or my will her eyes glaze over." One man told me he would wait until he and his wife were taking a long car ride so that he knew his wife couldn't leave, and then he would try to explain his business to her.

I believe that the best marriages are those in which there is financial sharing. Women have a right to know about their husband's money. It is not "cute" not to know.

There are no rules in the marriage game. There is no best way to discuss money. Nor is there a best way to manage money. Some couples like to work on the checkbook together. In some homes neither one wants to tackle the chore. The point here is that you have to discuss your plan and reach a joint decision about how you will do it. Who really likes balancing a checkbook anyway? It's not a privilege; it's a responsibility. The same is true for spending and investing your money. If you are wondering what happens in other families, women tend to play a leading role in day-to-day management of household finances but back away from long-term financial planning issues including taxes, insurance, and investments.[16]

Sometimes, a wife must take things into her own hands. One woman borrowed $1,500 from a friend to use as a down payment on a house worth $40,000. The real estate broker, a woman, introduced her to a lawyer, also a woman. She was the lawyer's first client. She didn't tell her husband. She used her own credit to obtain a 7½ percent mortgage and showed her husband that they would pay less as owners than they did as renters while also building equity. Her husband was so impressed he urged her to handle all their money.

Experts usually give a few rules for managing the family money. The principal one is to talk about it. If this always leads to the same old arguments maybe you should consider counseling to break the pattern. Set aside a special time to talk over your finances. Each couple must make its own way. We start out with a lot of cultural baggage about roles, about power, and even about ability. But marriage is also about sharing and trust and responsibility. In the past women knew their role as bread baker, not breadwinner. Women were not supposed to know about money. Remember Geraldine Ferraro, the first woman to run for vice president as a major party candidate? When her husband was accused of financial wrongdoing Ms. Ferraro, a lawyer and a savvy politician, said she was "just an Italian housewife"—her husband dealt with the money.

Today women and men have to redefine their roles. Instead of staying home, women work and bring home money in addition to taking care of their families. Marriage is supposed to be an economic partnership. Even if a woman is not bringing in the same amount, her contributions are important. Women must also take part in what was previously the man's domain, the finances. In the 1990s no woman should be ignorant about money— how it is earned, how it is spent, how it is invested. Knowing will not only help your marriage, but not knowing will leave you vulnerable while you are married and in trouble when you are no longer married.

And if you don't think this applies to you, just take a look at the facts.

HERE ARE SOME ABSOLUTELY FRIGHTENING STATISTICS YOU SHOULD STUDY NO MATTER HOW LONG YOU HAVE BEEN MARRIED, NO MATTER HOW HAPPY YOUR MARRIAGE:

- One third of all widows in 1985 were under age 50 when their husbands died.[17]
- Fifty percent of all women older than 65 in the United States are widows and will spend fifteen years as widows.[18]
- In 1992 there were 7,678,000 widows between the ages of 34 and 74. The average age of widowhood is 55.1.
- Four out of ten recent first marriages will end in divorce.[19]
- In 1975 the remarriage rate for divorced women aged 50 to 54 was 74 percent; in 1990, the remarriage rate was 63 percent.[20]
- Seventy-five percent of all nursing home occupants are women. (If he gets sick you will probably take care of him at home; you, however, will probably end up in a nursing home.)[21]

2.

I Do, I Do

Would you buy a house without reading the contract? Or take a job without knowing what you were expected to do, how many hours you would work, or what your salary would be? Probably not. Yet that is what you do when you sign a marriage license. Marriage is a legal contract between a man, a woman, and a third party—the state. Only states can issue marriage licenses, and these say very little about your marital rights. It's up to you and your husband to decide how you want to run your lives.

WOMEN, MARRIAGE, AND POWER: A BRIEF HISTORY

The role of the male as holder of power in a marriage goes back to the ancient Greeks and Romans. Marriage for the Greeks was governed by the need to protect the *oikos,* or family. The bride was given in marriage by her father. She was delivered over to the groom's house like a package. The husband became the keeper of his wife's property.

If she died, her sons got her property. Otherwise, it returned to her family.

The Romans continued this tradition. The term they used was *patria potestas.* So powerful was papa that he even had the right to kill his own sons. Women had far lower status, which is not to say that some of them didn't have great influence. Our word *marriage* comes originally from the Latin *maritus,* which means "provided with a bride." In the Roman marriage ritual, as depicted on Roman coins, the couples joined their right hands in a ceremony presided over by Concordia, the goddess who symbolized the union of citizens.

When Christianity began to replace the pagan empire, the Roman concept of marriage was simply incorporated into the new rites, but with a slight variation. Christ was now seen presiding over the marriage, and the bride and groom would no longer clasp hands. This has been seen as a change from a contractual idea to one of marriage as a more spiritual union.

The early Christian husband nevertheless assumed control of the wife's estate at marriage and accepted the concurrent obligation to provide support and maintenance during the marriage. The traditional Anglo-Saxon wedding didn't do much to change things. The ceremonial words used implied a giving of the bride to the husband. The wife and husband were then assumed to be one unit. This identity was further supported by the wife's assumption of her husband's name.

Until recently in America, women who married gave up their rights. During the colonial and revolutionary periods a husband had "control over the real property [land and buildings] a wife brought into marriage. He could use this property as he pleased but could not sell or give it away because it descended to his wife's legal heirs."[1] The law, however, gave him ownership of his wife's personal property—including her wages. These he could dispose of as he saw fit.

By the middle of the nineteenth century married women were making gains. In 1924 the League of Women Voters could proclaim "sixteen states [give] women an absolute right of contract, without any restrictions."[2] Today married women have the same rights as single women or men. A woman can make contracts, own property, and have credit in her own name.

Through the nineteenth century, because women gave up rights, they gained certain protections. Your husband had to support and maintain you. He was responsible for debts you had before you married and was responsible for "necessaries." Necessaries were defined as food, clothing, shelter, and medical needs. If your husband didn't provide food for you and the children he would then be liable to a merchant who gave you those items. These laws were written at a time when a wife had no recourse: She couldn't easily divorce. There was little she could do. The laws were written to protect the merchant who might help the indigent wife. In exchange for these guarantees, wives became dependent. Today state marriage laws are written in the new legal language that talks about "spouses" and equality. Courts have taken the position that "both spouses should be jointly held liable for each other's necessaries." Until the middle of this century a wife could not sue or be sued except through her husband. Nor could a wife sue her husband because that would have been like suing herself. This is a legal concept known as spousal immunity that is only gradually changing.

MARRIAGE LAWS AND MARITAL RIGHTS TODAY

Nothing in the marriage laws of the fifty American states mandates, for a spouse who does not bring in his or her own income, a minimum amount of spending money, a minimum sized home, a car, or anything else. It is only obligatory that each provide the other with "necessaries." Most states would also uphold each partner's marital right to sexual relations. Failure to engage in marital sex could lead to a charge of "constructive abandonment" or a "failure to fulfill this basic obligation of marriage." These are rights that are not specifically legislated but have come down through judicial interpretation, our so-called "common law."

This common law or law by tradition is the concept that also underlies common law marriage. Only thirteen states recognize a marriage that is not licensed.* The criteria for such marriages is the mutual agreement of man and woman that they will live as husband and wife. If you enter into a common law marriage in a state where it is valid, then other states must recognize it too. If you

---

*Alabama, Colorado, Georgia, Idaho, Iowa, Kansas, Montana, Ohio, Oklahoma, Pennsylvania, Rhode Island, South Carolina, Texas, and Washington, D.C.

establish a common law marriage, the rules for splitting up are the same as if you had gone ahead and gotten the license. Should you want to claim your marital rights, either in a divorce or under a will, you are probably better off having had a legal marriage.

The federal government plays a limited role in the laws of marriage. Pensions are regulated by federal laws and federal laws now mandate that women have a right to share in their husbands' pension funds, even if they didn't work. Federal laws supersede state laws in areas such as bankruptcy and federal taxes. These days both federal and state laws are constantly changing. If you are contemplating any significant changes in your life be sure you know the law, because what follows throughout the book is a general summary. Husbands, of course, can share in the pensions their wives receive. The federal government has also eliminated taxes on transfers of wealth between husband and wife.

Each state has its own qualifications for obtaining a marriage license. There are age restrictions. In Georgia you can marry at sixteen but you must have parental consent. If you are pregnant or already have a child, the age restrictions are waived. In New York you can marry as young as fourteen if your parents consent. There are restrictions on whom you can marry. Unlike Cleopatra, you cannot marry your brother. In some states you can't even marry (Habsburgs take note) your first cousin. But it's okay in California. Should you be greedy enough to want two husbands at the same time, the state will again say no. Should you be tying the knot for the second time, you will have to explain what you did with your first husband. Some states have a waiting period between the issuing of the license and the actual marriage ceremony. In Indiana you can even get married over the telephone, since both parties need not be present for the ceremony.[3] Most states have medical requirements. You may need a blood test. In California you may need a test for German measles if you are under the age of fifty.

Other than the cost of the license ($30 for New York City) there are no financial requirements. There are also no financial guarantees. Should you contemplate ending your marriage by divorce, you will discover that you have some very specific rights.

Should your husband die without a will, your right to inherit his property is clearly spelled out, again according to the laws of the state in which you live. For example, if you and your husband have no children you would receive three quarters of his property in Indiana, and one quarter would go to his parents if they were still alive. In Kentucky you would receive half of your husband's estate and the rest would go to his parents if they were still alive. In West Virginia you would inherit all your husband's property even if his parents were still alive.

Should your husband die and leave a will, each state spells out the minimum amount of his property that must be left to you, regardless of what the will says. This is known as your "dower" right, or forced share. Again it derives from Anglo-Saxon tradition. You had certain income rights that could not be taken away.

In fact, it is illegal for a man to disinherit his wife, although he can disinherit his children, except in Louisiana. Your husband also has rights to inherit from you, known as "curtesy." This too can be traced to Anglo-Saxon origins.

The most important determinant of your rights is the state in which you live. Nine states—Arizona, California, Idaho, Louisiana, New Mexico, Oregon, Texas, Washington, and Wisconsin—are community property states, which means you each own half of all the property you both amass during the marriage, regardless of who earns it or whose name is on the title. Wisconsin is a community property state, except for division of assets in a divorce. All the other states adhere to common law. Common law is not rigid and fixed but relies instead on broad principles, supposedly based on reason and common sense.

Our laws derive from two different traditions. Common law derives from the Anglo-Saxon idea that merged husband and wife into one entity and gave the husband all the power. He owned all the property and the wife became almost totally dependent.

In common law states the key to ownership of property during marriage depends on whose name is on the title. The titleholder has the right to sell the property or mortgage it, even if it is the home where you live. You do not have a right to your husband's earnings nor he to yours, except the right that each of you has to provide necessaries for each other. If your husband is the wage earner, he has control over his wages. He can dole out the money as he chooses.

The community property tradition comes from Spain—really from the Visigothic tribes that settled Spain. Supposedly, Visigoth men and women were partners who shared their rugged migratory life. The partnership meant that each partner owned half the property. But the Spanish, who were landowners, also wanted to protect the land, so they added their own stamp—the idea of separate property. If you entered the marriage with land, that land remained yours.

Community property means each spouse owns a one-half interest in any property acquired during the marriage, (except property that was inherited or received as a gift). Both husband and wife have the right to control the community property during marriage. This means that the consent of husband and wife would be required to pledge or sell any community property. California goes even further and states that a woman can spend 100 percent of her husband's community property share, but not land; both of you have to consent to sell real estate. You don't have to ask if you want to sell his yacht. Of course, he has the same right to spend yours.

Regardless of whether you live in a community property or a common property state, property is either considered marital property or separate property. These distinctions may not seem significant in a good marriage where you share your resources, but could become important under some circumstances.

For example, in a common law state, if you do not work and want a credit card, you must rely on your husband's credit, but in a community property state, if you do not work and want a credit card, half your husband's marital assets, including his salary, are considered your property. On the other hand, in a community property state you and your husband are jointly responsible for debts, even if only your husband signed the credit card. If the marriage ends and your husband had a pile of debts, they would be considered half yours. In a common law state, the debts would be his.

Your engagement ring is not marital property; it is a gift to you. It is your separate property. If you break the engagement, etiquette suggests you return it. As for wedding gifts, they were traditionally considered the property of the bride. In the new spirit of sharing, the wedding gifts are considered to be jointly owned—that is, unless a gift was clearly given to the bride or groom. In fact, a South Carolina court recently decided that a silver tea service, given by the bride's grandmother as a wedding present, was not marital property.[4] So you probably won't have to split the bridal negligee.

Just ask Abraham Ullah about the meaning of marital property. Mr. Ullah, a Brooklyn resident, purchased a $1 lottery ticket in 1986. His ticket came in—to the tune of $8 million. Both Ullah and his wife quit their jobs. Soon after, they filed for divorce. Mr. Ullah claimed the entire $8 million as his because he had purchased the ticket and picked the winning numbers. Furthermore, his wife was opposed to gambling. The judge in Brooklyn Supreme Court saw things differently and gave Mrs. Ullah half the winnings. Mr. Ullah appealed the decision, but the appellate court judge said the winnings were won "on a wager of a marital dollar."[5]

The New York Equitable Distribution Statute, known as Domestic Relations Law 236, defines the term as follows: "The term marital property shall mean all property acquired by either or both spouses during the marriage and before the execution of a separation agreement or the commencement of a matrimonial action, regardless of the form in which title is held . . . Marital property shall not include separate property as hereinafter defined. . . ." If you are working, your salary earned while you are married is marital property. If your husband buys a house with money he earned while you are married, the house is marital property.

The difference between owning that house in a community property state or a common law state is that during the marriage you are not a one-half owner of the house in a common law state unless your husband wants you to be. In a community property state such as California, the law requires that you are a half owner.

Separate property, at least according to the New York State code, is considered:

(1) property acquired before marriage or property acquired by bequest, devise, or descent, and gift from a party other than the spouse;
(2) compensation for personal injuries;
(3) property acquired in exchange for or the increase in value of separate property, except to the extent that such appreciation is due in part to the contributions of efforts of the other spouse;
(4) property described as separate property by written agreement of the parties . . .

If you owned a house before your marriage the house is your separate property. If you were hit by a truck and collected $100,000 that money is yours. If you bought a house with that money, the house is yours. If you and your husband signed a prenuptial agreement that clearly stated that the house is yours, then it's yours. However, if the house appreciates in value, that appreciation can become marital property. While this may seem simple, it is not. When you marry in a community property state, you and your husband split fifty-fifty everything that is earned during the marriage.

On the other hand, debts also become community property. If your husband borrows money that he then blows at a casino in Nevada, half the debt is yours. In a common law state, if he goes to the casino and loses, the debt is his. If you have a credit card and your husband uses it, the debt is yours.

In a common law state, death, divorce, or separation activates your rights.

In Arizona, Idaho, Nevada, Texas, and Wisconsin the laws change slightly about property division in a divorce—and division of property is based also on your ability to work, your age, etc. In Washington, community property laws apply during marriage and at death but upon divorce the courts may consider all property in making a division.

While this might not seem important in the throes of first love, consider what could happen: If you have no property in your name and you die, in a common law state you would have nothing to leave in your will for your parents or other relatives you might want to support. What if you die in an accident? Despite the best medical treatment, you do not survive. Your husband is distraught. He turns for comfort to a lovely divorcée. They marry. You had always planned to support your elderly mother, but of course you had no property to leave to her. What will your husband and his new wife do for her?

The point of this story is that if you live in a common law state and your home is owned in your husband's name, you will have nothing to leave to your mother. Had you lived in a community property state, half the house, even if your husband had earned all the money, would have been yours. You could have left your half to your mother.

If you live in a common law state, you don't automatically own half the property. You have to specify joint ownership when you buy it, and you should know the different types before you do. They are:

- *Joint Tenancy with Right of Survivorship.* Each of you owns the property. If one of you dies, the property goes to the other. This type of ownership would not help you if you wanted to leave your half of your house to your mother.
- *Joint Tenancy by the Entirety.* This is the same as above, only limited to ownership by husbands and wives—i.e., you must be married to qualify.
- *Joint Tenancy in Common.* This is closest to the type of ownership you would have in a community property state. You each own half the property and can leave your half in whatever way you choose. This is the best way to be sure your half of the house goes to your old mother.

Don't assume that the law will protect you. In the past few years state laws have changed drastically. For a long time laws were written to protect the family as a single legal entity with the husband as its head. The courts could not easily invade the sanctity of the home. But today the courts allow individual identity even within a marriage. You and your husband have separate rights, such as the right to have credit in your own name. While there are laws to govern asset distribution when you die or divorce, no legislation exists in common law states to control finances as long as a marriage is intact.

Should you divorce in a common law state, the law will

consider the property you and your husband acquired during your marriage "marital" property—to be divided. However, during the marriage the property is legally controlled by the spouse who earned the money. Often the majority of that money is earned by the husband. Sharing of that money during marriage must come from a private decision by husband and wife.

How you handle money and make financial decisions may be one of the important decisions you will make in your marriage. A willingness to share financially is really a part of the mutual trust that underlies a good marriage. The best time to plan what you will do is in the beginning. That is when you will, especially if you are marrying for the first time, have the least amount of money and be most willing to compromise. Knowing that you have some legal rights to your husband's money, and he to yours, can help you to participate in the family finances.

You may want to make some decisions with the help of your lawyer, especially if you are starting over (approximately 45 percent of recent marriages have one spouse who was previously wed). You may want a prenuptial agreement (see Chapter 4). This is nothing more than a contract, something a marriage license doesn't provide.

If you are already married—and this especially applies to women who are in long marriages—have never worked, and have been financially dependent on your husband, you should know as much about the family finances as possible. While there is no one way to handle the marital finances, there are a few things you might want to consider.

TEN FINANCIAL RULES FOR MARRIAGE

1. Show him your finances. Naturally you'll expect to see his.
2. Don't forget to examine his debts, especially in community property states where you might both have to pay for each other's old debts. You should each check your credit ratings.* A bad loan in the past could mean trouble. One couple could not get a mortgage because he had skipped out on his student loan.
3. Decide whether or not you want to pool your assets. Making a conscious—and mutual—decision about this is highly recommended for first marriages.
4. Decide who will pay for what and how. When one of you makes much more than the other you may not be able to split expenses down the middle. One couple, in which the wife had more money than the husband, agreed that she would pay for certain things, but the husband never felt comfortable if his wife paid in public. So they arranged for him to always be the one who paid when they went out. Then the wife would reimburse him.

---

*To obtain a copy of your credit report you must contact the credit rating bureau that serves your area. The main credit bureaus are TRW Information Services (P.O. Box 2350, Chatsworth, Calif. 91313, 1-800-392-1122), Trans Union Credit Information (760 Sproul Road, Springfield, Penn. 19064, 1-800-462-8054), and Equifax, Inc. (P.O. Box 105873, Atlanta, Ga. 30374, 1-800-685-1111). You may have to pay a small charge for your report. If you have been denied credit based on the bureau's report within the previous thirty days you are entitled to a free report. Most agencies require a written request, including your Social Security number, your birthdate, and current and previous residences. Include any required fee.

5. When only one of you earns the money, that one should not necessarily make all the decisions. Financial decisions should be joint.

6. No matter how you split finances and who earns what, make sure you each have some discretionary funds. One wife told me she had always managed her own finances before she married. When she married she and her husband decided on a joint checking account. Everything went into it. She hated having her husband know and question every expense. Things really got touchy when her husband questioned a hairdresser's bill that was large. He asked, "Why did you spend all that money? You don't look any different." She wisely replied, "That shows what a good job it was," and demanded her own account for personal expenses.

7. If you have separate property, think very carefully about whether you want to put it in a joint account. It's easy to give up control to show that you trust somebody. But you may regret it in the future. There is nothing wrong with having your own money.

8. Read the tax returns and ask questions. Don't worry about sounding ignorant. How else will you learn? You should speak to the accountant, too.

9. Never sign a contract that you don't understand.

10. Keep records—of everything. (See Chapter 3 for details on what to keep.)

3.
Marriage, Inc.

I remember my first wedding. I remember the shocking-pink wool suit I wore for the ceremony; I remember the Raphael, the small Paris hotel with a view of the Eiffel Tower where we went on our wedding trip; and I remember all eight wedding guests. But there is little I could have told you about our finances in those early days. Nobody should be as naïve as I was. Eight years later my husband died and I was alone with a one-year-old baby. It took me two years to even understand that I could not afford to live in the house that I owned.

Yet what happened to me isn't that extraordinary. Any woman married today is likely to fall victim to one of what I call The Three D's: Death, Divorce, or other Disasters. If you are married now, your odds of being alone are high.

Recently, Betsy, a research librarian, became suspicious that her husband of twenty years was going to leave her. Before she could be sure, her husband had already spirited much of what she thought of as the family assets out of the country and into a Bahamian bank account. Although Betsy had signed joint tax returns, she had no idea exactly how much money her husband earned a year. Nor, to be perfectly fair, did she know how much money she spent. She didn't have a clue about the family finances.

Even if she never thought about divorce, she should have known about the money that was coming in and going out. In fact, one of the problems of the marriage was her refusal to stop spending money when her husband's business was losing money.

When it comes to knowing about the family money, most women probably fall somewhere between Betsy, who knew nothing, and those women we all know who handle all the family finances. Some of us may know our husband's salary, but not realize how much he has put into his pension plan; others may know all about the investments, but not realize how much the health insurance costs, because that is deducted from your husband's salary.

FIVE THINGS WOMEN DON'T USUALLY KNOW ABOUT THEIR HUSBAND'S MONEY

1. How much he has and how much he owes
2. How the assets are held (savings accounts, property, stocks, etc.)
3. How much insurance he has and what kind
4. How much he spends
5. How he's leaving it (the will)

There are two ways to discover the facts about your husband's finances. The good way is by sharing throughout the marriage. The other, and less pleasant, way is when financial disaster strikes and you discover that you are in debt, have worthless investments, or even face bankruptcy.

Studies have shown that women tend to abdicate a role in investment decisions. This is probably one of the biggest money mistakes any woman can make. Where is the evidence that men are better money managers? Even if you have had little experience in investing, you can learn. Take a course, read, and rely on your own common sense. Most of the time you will do as well as your husband, if not better. The big difference is probably that you don't think you can, or that you don't think you have a right to. You can, you do, and you should.

Of course, some women never find out about the facts of their husbands' finances until the marriage dissolves tragically—in divorce or death. Mary Elizabeth Murray, a retired schoolteacher, learned the hard way after her husband died. He had managed the investments, and when he died she let the broker handle her account. Before long Mrs. Murray had lost $125,000. Without asking her, the broker had sold her blue-chip securities and bought risky investments. Mrs. Murray took her case to an arbitration committee and was awarded $419,460. But it was a painful way to learn about investing.[1]

One way to begin learning about your husband's money, and your own, is to think of your family as a small corporation. Don't think that this means you have to have millions in the bank. It is merely a way to look at what you do have.

Corporations, large and small, generally prepare two types of reports. One is a net worth statement, the other a cash flow statement. Your net worth is really a record of what you have and what you owe—your assets and liabilities on a particular day. Corporations usually do an annual net worth report, but asset values such as stock prices can change quickly, so the net worth applies only to the day on which it is calculated. The cash flow statement lets you see how much money is coming in every month or year and how much is going out—in other words, income and expenses.

Start with a look at what you have. If you and your husband pool everything, you only need one, but you should include in your list how each asset is owned. If you have separate assets you may want to have separate accounts. If you don't want to approach your husband do it on your own. (See chart pages 34–35.)

Corporate financial reports also include what is called a cash flow statement: this really means the spendable income—the amount of cash you have coming in, and the amount of cash going out. If these two are not equal and the amount going out is greater than that coming in, you are spending too much. (See chart pages 36–37.)

The amount of money you and your husband spend is extremely important. Yet we go into marriage—or, for that matter, live on our own—with few rules about spending. One marriage I know of nearly broke up because the husband and wife could not agree on their spending. Nancy and Don are probably like many couples. Nancy turned over her paycheck to Don, who paid most of the bills. Nancy had a checking account that she used for everyday expenses. One day Nancy noticed a bank statement on Don's desk. She discovered that Don had taken a $10,000 loan to buy a camper. When Don came home

How to Calculate Your Net Worth[*]

ASSETS

Personal Property:
  house
  furniture and household effects (e.g., a wine collection, a
    library of books, compact disks)
  appliances, machines, and tools
  car, boat
Financial Assets:
  commodities
  stocks
  bonds
  checking and savings accounts
  mutual funds, money market funds, CDs
Real Estate
Business Partnerships
Hidden Assets:
  stock options
  pension funds, Keogh, IRA, SEP
  insurance (cash and benefit value)
  possible inheritance
  deferred compensation (money you have earned but will
    receive in the future)

[*]Your net worth is the difference between your assets and your liabilities.

that evening she asked him about the loan. In the argument that ensued, Nancy discovered that she and Don had been living way over their incomes. Nancy even feared they could go bankrupt if they were to have any unexpected expenses.

Don thought Nancy was overreacting. After all, he explained, everything worked out perfectly when he ran the numbers through his computer. Don had used the

How to Calculate Your Net Worth *(Cont.)*

LIABILITIES

Outstanding Taxes:
  Social Security
  federal
  state and local
  real estate
Mortgages
Loans:
  business
  personal
  car
  home equity
Credit Card Debt
Installment Debt
Margin Debt on Stock Brokerage Accounts

---

computer to control and intimidate Nancy. Her fear of being in debt finally overcame her fear of challenging Don and the computer. "Everything was on the computer—it was his security," Nancy recalled. But not this time. After years of being intimidated by the authority that the computer numbers seemed to represent, Nancy demanded an accounting that she could understand—with pencil and paper.

How to Calculate Your Expenses

INCOME

Salary
Bonus
Dividends
Partnership Interest
Trust Income
Rental Income
Interest Income
   savings accounts
   money market funds
   CDs
Alimony

OUTGO

Mortgage and Amortization
   household repairs
   real estate taxes
Taxes and Charges
Debt Service on Credit Cards and Loans
Utilities:
   fuel and gas
   electricity
   telephone
Food and Liquor
Personal Care:
   hairdresser and health club
   books and magazines
Clothing:
   laundry
   dry cleaner
Automobile:
   fuel
   repairs
   insurance
   car payments

How to Calculate Your Expenses *(Cont.)*

OUTGO
_____

Insurance:
  life
  personal and real property
  fire, theft, and liability
  medical/dental
  disability
  nursing home
Travel and Entertainment:
  nonreimbursed expenses
  reimbursed expenses
Vacations
Children:
  tuition
  child care
  clothing
Charity:
  religious organizations
  museum contributions
  alumnae associations
  health organizations
Savings and Investments
Miscellaneous Expenses:
  cigarettes
  office coffee breaks
  newspapers and magazines
  cosmetics
  (and don't forget those vet bills for Fido)
Alimony and Child Support

When Nancy began going over their expenses she realized that Don had developed a pattern of overspending. Each year he paid off the previous year's debts with his year-end bonus, but somehow the debts were never totally wiped out. They never started the year with a clean slate. With Don's company in financial trouble, there was a good chance that he wouldn't even get a bonus this year. Then what would they do?

Nancy took over the finances, including the checkbook. She cut their expenses to the bone, putting them both on a food and clothing allowance. Gradually, over a six-month period, she began to cut their debt and their tendency to overspend. Don now admits that for the first time he no longer feels out of control. They are still vulnerable if a major disaster should hit them—say, needing a new roof for the house or a new car—but Nancy thinks they are on the right track.

The problem Nancy faced is not unusual. As in most of what we do in marriage, there are few guidelines. Spending just seems to happen. But it doesn't have to be like that.

CAN YOU AFFORD IT?

It's easy to figure out how much to spend. You just have to know that you can't pay out more than what comes in. The trouble is: credit. You can always buy just a little more than you can actually pay for, thanks to those little plastic credit cards. The problem comes when you find yourself charging on three or four cards. No one card will get you in trouble, but together they can begin to make a big dent in your monthly expenses. Add that to mortgages and car loans and pretty soon you could be like Nancy's husband, Don—totally out of control, but under the illusion that everything is all right because you've put all the numbers in your computer.

What follows are some guidelines. If Nancy had known these figures she might have had the courage to stop Don before they had big problems. While most families have slightly different needs at different times, you might want to compare your family spending with those of other American families. (See below.)

But Nancy really needs to know more than average expenses. She also should know how much debt is consid-

AVERAGE BREAKDOWN OF EXPENSES
IN AMERICAN FAMILIES[2]

TYPE OF EXPENSE	PERCENTAGE OF TOTAL EXPENSES
FOOD:	14.4
at home	8.9
away from home	5.5
HOUSING	31.8
APPAREL AND SERVICES	5.7
TRANSPORTATION:	17.5
vehicles	7.3
gasoline and motor oil	3.3
other transportation	6.9
HEALTH CARE	5.5
INSURANCE AND PENSIONS:	9.2
life and other personal insurance	1.2
pensions and Social Security	8.0
ENTERTAINMENT	5.0
OTHER EXPENDITURES	11.0

ered tolerable. Even though Nancy thinks the only good debt is one that has been paid, Don is right to borrow money. It's one way to build assets. The problem with Don's borrowing was that it was going more to luxury goods—fancy restaurants and expensive suits and vacations—than it was toward building assets.

Debt payments for a family should be 35 percent of your gross monthly income, which would include 25 percent for mortgage and housing expenses. But first you should have on hand enough liquid assets for three to six months of living expenses.

There are several computer programs that can help you keep track of all this information, but all you really need is a pencil and paper. You don't even need a calculator.

One of the most important reasons for knowing all the facts and figures is to be able to know what you would need if something happened to your husband. If you were left alone because of divorce or death, how would you manage? If you don't know now, you'll really have problems later on.

SHARING INCOME, EXPENSES, AND DEBTS

Not knowing about marital finances leaves you out of control of the situation. Yet many women like Nancy abdicate their financial role and let their husbands take over. Sometimes women do this because it's easier, because taking charge is taking responsibility. Sometimes women let their husbands take over because they feel they don't have the right to participate since they don't earn the money. Yet, in most cases, sharing the financial burden, either because you each earn some of the money or because you both decide and are responsible for the way money is spent, can improve marriages.

There are two kinds of money in marriage: first, the money that you and your husband earn and spend, your income, and second, the investments or other assets that you and your husband own and manage. You and your husband have to decide how you want to own and share your income and assets. If you live in a community property state, the state decides ownership for you; the assets and income you acquire during your marriage are owned jointly. But if you live in a common law state, the income or assets are owned by the person whose name is on the title.

There really isn't a best way to own assets or spend money. A lawyer who has seen many couples argue viciously about money during a divorce might advocate separate ownership of all property. A psychologist who has seen couples argue endlessly about money during their marriage might say that unless the assets are merged there will never be a true marriage.

At different times in your life you may want to do things differently. When I married my first husband we had few assets. We each earned a small salary, although his was much higher than mine. We shared everything. We owned our house jointly and we pooled our income. When I married for the second time, I had a child from my first marriage. My husband had his own family obligations. We also each had separate property. We have a much more complicated financial arrangement. As in most second marriages, not all of our expenses are joint.

(In 1992, according to the Department of Health, there were 2.3 million weddings. Of these, 10.7 percent were divorced men who married never-married women; 10.9 percent were divorced women and never-married men.[3]) Who actually writes the rent check or manages the stock portfolio may not be important at all, but you should both know what is going on. Most young couples in first marriages will probably share everything, so joint ownership is the most logical, regardless of who earns what. After all, isn't sharing why you got married? If you both work, you can share major expenses, share savings, and each keep some separate money for your own expenses.

If you have joint checking accounts and credit cards you should still have a credit card in your own name and a separate checking account, even if you have agreed to share all expenses.

If you do not have a credit card in your own name but have a joint card with your husband, you can have your credit report in both names. You must request this when you apply for the card. That way, you will begin establishing your own credit history. If your account is old, you may have to write to the company to request a change in the way your credit is reported. If you have your own credit history, you can more easily get a credit card in your own name should you want one. If you are widowed and do not have earned income, obtaining a credit card can be difficult. You are better off having your own card before anything happens. If your husband is a bad credit risk, you definitely want only your own credit cards, not a joint account.

I had charge accounts in my husband's name and continued using them after my husband died. Nobody told me not to, and as long as I continued to pay my bills on time, I didn't have a problem. However, I felt insecure until I was able to change the cards into my own name. If you are only authorized to sign your husband's credit card, he can easily cancel it should you get divorced. One woman told of being totally humiliated in the small town where she lived when she went to the drugstore and was told her husband had closed the account. If you have a joint checking account, all the more reason to keep a separate checking account as well because he can clean out the account if he is planning a divorce.

As for responsibility for debts, each state differs. For example the California law says that you could even be responsible for some debts your husband had before marriage. In Maryland, however, neither spouse is liable for the other's debts incurred before marriage.

To Have and to Hold

Here is what you should absolutely keep handy in the house (I do this on one sheet of paper):

• Social Security numbers
• bank account numbers
• brokerage account numbers
• money market fund numbers
• insurance policy numbers

- credit card numbers (handy for catalogue ordering late at night and more important for reporting stolen cards)

I also keep all the numbers for our airline travel mileage so I can always tell the reservation clerk numbers when I make plane reservations.

Here is what you should keep close by:

- tax returns (last seven years)
- W-2 forms
- brokerage account statements (I keep the monthly statements for the current year and the yearly statements for the past seven years)
- bank statements (canceled checks are always a problem—I keep a year's worth handy and store seven years of back checks)
- insurance policies—homeowners insurance, health insurance, life insurance
- copy of your will (original can be kept at your lawyer's office)
- inventory of all your possessions

Here is what you should keep in a safety deposit box:

- property deeds
- car title
- any IOUs
- marriage license
- divorce papers
- leases
- stocks and bonds

MONEY MISTAKES WOMEN MAKE[4]

While there are no rules for deciding how you and your husband should divide your money, many women who entered marriage thinking they would somehow work out the money without talking about it discovered years later that they had made some terrible mistakes. Below are nine common ones to avoid.

1. *Putting inherited money or property in a joint account.* Recently, my friends' daughter married. As a wedding gift, her parents gave the couple a house. This was very good, except for one thing: The new husband's first wife used this property as an excuse to try to get more money from her ex-husband. Keeping the house in the daughter's name would have simplified the situation.

2. *Using her money for expenses while her husband's investments increased.* For nine of the thirteen years of her marriage, Linda outearned her husband. They split expenses and used her extra earnings to pay taxes. Sounds reasonable. But all the time they were using her money, his separate investment account, which he had before they married, continued to grow.

3. *Not getting professional advice soon enough.* Remember Betsy, whose husband put the family assets into a Bahamian bank account? By the time Betsy thought to go to a divorce lawyer, her husband had set up investments that her lawyer was never able to find.

4. *Giving up control over her money to show faith and to*

bolster her husband's ego. Diane's husband took charge of the family finances, mainly her salary, while she worked and he stayed home. Too late she discovered that he put them in debt. She was stuck for the loans.

5. *Letting him keep all the family records.* When she and her husband divorced, Elaine didn't have the money to find out what there was, where it was, or how much it was worth.

6. *Trying to pay an equal share when she couldn't really afford to do so.* Esther's husband was much richer than Esther was. Yet they agreed to split everything. Problems developed when she lost her big earning job and dipped into her savings to try to keep up her end. She spent all her money, and because it was a second marriage had little to leave for her children from her first marriage.

7. *Using her separate money to buy something in joint name while her husband holds on to his separate investments.* When they split, Abby's husband got half the joint property, Abby got none of his separate investments.

8. *Not keeping records or receipts—especially for cash payments.* Gwen's husband was hiding income. She couldn't prove this and when they divorced she received a settlement based on his understated tax returns.

9. *The biggest mistake of all—thinking that talking about money is not romantic.* The very precautions that would help you at the time of a divorce or the death of your husband—prenuptial agreements, accurate records about property, knowing the value of stock

options—are viewed as unromantic. Not talking about money could lead to most of the above eight problems.

While many of these problems led to divorce, they were often problems that, handled differently, might have been resolved. In Diane's case, her husband plunged them into debt. Had they made joint decisions, they would probably still be married. But she began to lose faith in him when she saw how he handled what she had always thought of as their money.

The friend who paid an equal share of the expenses even though her husband was much richer began to resent every penny she had to give her husband. And frequently, it was pennies. When they went on a trip he would even record every bus fare in his little book. The final rupture came when he suggested that they invite her mother for dinner and then divided the check, one third, two thirds.

A possible divorce is not the only reason you should know about money, how it is spent, where it is kept, how it is invested, and how it is owed. It is equally important if you are widowed. Otherwise you will become a victim of what I have heard called "widowitis." Its chief symptom is the fear that ensues from not knowing what you can afford to do when you are on your own and not knowing how to do it.

But even more important, not knowing about the family money can leave you in a marriage in which you do not play an equal role in making decisions. It can leave you feeling dependent and vulnerable. Knowing about the assets, helping to keep the records, helping to make the decisions are all part of the economic partnership that modern marriage is supposed to be.

4.
"Honey, Just Sign Here"

When the history of New York in the 1980s is written, Donald and Ivana Trump will loom large as the quintessential twosome: she, a ravishing blonde from Czechoslovakia who wore beautiful clothes; he, a tall, brash real estate developer who owned hotels and gambling casinos. Magazines fed the public a continuous diet of Trump style. We saw their glittering triplex apartment, their yacht, and their palatial Palm Beach mansion. We knew their charities and their friends. We saw their helicopter whisking them to fabulous parties. What we didn't see was a young blonde from Georgia. When the papers broke the news of the Trumps' marital split, the banner headlines dwarfed those given to African leader Nelson Mandela, released after twenty years in prison.

While much was made of Mr. Trump's liaison with another woman, the main focus of the press was the revelation of the couple's premarital agreement. Details were quickly leaked alleging that Mrs. Trump was to receive $25 million, their Connecticut mansion, and custody of the children. Various sources further disclosed that the agreement, which had been written at the time of their marriage, had been revised three times since. His lawyers declared the agreement "ironclad"; her lawyers called it "unconscionable" and "fraudulent." Marital behavior that might have caused Mr. Trump to relinquish a large part of his fortune in the past was of no consequence. What counted was the premarital contract. In the end, you could not feel sorry for Ivana. She walked away with $10 million, a forty-five-room Connecticut mansion, a New York apartment, and use of the couple's 118-room Mar-a-Lago mansion in Florida for one month a year. And to be sure, the kids are okay; she gets $650,000 per year in alimony and child support.

Prenuptial agreements have been around for a long time. The Babylonians had them in the first millennium B.C. The agreements spelled out the dowry the bride would bring with her as well as the settlement should the marriage end in divorce. Often the inheritance rights of any children of the marriage were included. Agreements even allowed the wife's dowry to return to her father's estate should she die without children.

When Elizabeth I of England contemplated marriage, her agents tried to hammer out an agreement with the agents for the duke of Alençon, a Frenchman twenty years her junior. In June of 1579, Alençon's agents crossed the channel to work out the contract. They demanded the duke be crowned king immediately after the wedding, that a large pension be paid to him throughout his life, and that he would have the right to remain a practicing Catholic. The queen's agents asked Alençon to foreswear any contribution toward expenses should France go to war against the Netherlands. Queen Bess needed more than a lawyer; the entire Privy Council had to agree. They didn't and the marriage never took place.

In America, premarital agreements were considered the domain of the very rich, who used them mainly to limit the amount of money a husband or wife could inherit. Prior to the 1970s the courts would not uphold an agreement that spelled out conditions in the event of a divorce. Women were not allowed to waive their rights to alimony (it would have been unthinkable for men to receive alimony). Remember, property usually went to the owner—usually the husband—so alimony was the only point of negotiation in a divorce settlement. This was a way of protecting the little woman and preventing her from becoming a public charge.

Courts also worried that prenuptial contracts—also called antenuptial contracts—that waived alimony promoted divorce, because the husband would have no obligations if he left. But now that it's okay for women to work and for women to be considered equal, support is no longer a concern of the law.

Premarital agreements crop up everywhere these days, including the corporate world. When James Stewart, former chairman of Lone Star Industries, Inc., married one of his five wives, he billed the company $16,795 in legal fees for his prenuptial agreement and was reimbursed. When Charles Lazarus, who made a fortune as chief of Toys "R" Us, was accused by a shareholder of violating an obscure stock exchange trading rule, he denied the allegations. His explanation: The stock was owned by his wife, sex therapist Helen Kaplan, and they had a prenuptial agreement which kept her money separate from his. The court agreed with him.

The advent of equitable distribution laws, a rise in the divorce rate, a high number of second marriages, and an increase in the number of working women with their own assets have increased the number of prenuptial agreements. Many couples use the prenuptial agreement as a marriage contract, spelling out the consequences of a breakup or death much the way partners in a business would sign a contract. You might look at a prenuptial agreement as the economic contract of a marriage. All too often, however, it is an agreement made between unequals.

Prenuptial agreements are subject to state law. Many states have adopted a variation of the 1983 Uniform Premarital Agreement Act. States that have not adopted the Uniform Act have enacted some form of similar legislation which outlines the conditions under which an agreement should be signed, the settlement of property, and the conditions under which an agreement may not be enforceable. Check your state. In some, agreements must be notarized to be valid.

What You Give Up When You Sign a Prenuptial Agreement

If you are getting married and your husband-to-be wants you to sign such an agreement, there are a few things you should know. Under the laws of the various states, you as the wife are legally entitled to certain "fruits" of the marriage should it end either in death or divorce. When you sign an agreement, you may give up some or all of these rights depending on the terms of the agreement.

1. You may be giving up your right to inherit property under your husband's will or under the intestate (having made no valid will) laws of your state. You are also giving up your elective share (the minimum amount of assets your husband must leave to you).
2. You may be giving up your right to an equitable distribution or a community property settlement should your marriage end in divorce.
3. You may be giving up other rights to which you are entitled in your state, such as the right to receive support, should your marriage end in divorce.
4. Some states also have homestead laws that would permit you to stay in the family home should you and your husband divorce.

If you are the one asking for an agreement, your husband is giving up the same rights to your assets. A prenuptial agreement supersedes state laws. When a Nebraska husband recently tried to claim his "elective" share under his wife's will, even though he had signed a prenuptial agreement, the courts ruled against him. The terms of the prenuptial agreement prevailed.

HOW PRENUPTIAL AGREEMENTS STAND UP

Most state courts will uphold prenuptial agreements, providing they do not leave one spouse destitute (known as the public policy issue). Nor do some state laws permit agreements that are thought to facilitate divorce. For example, the courts would not uphold an agreement that required you and your husband to divorce in five years. A Utah judge recently overturned an agreement because he said it was "against public policy to facilitate the breakup of a marital relationship."[1]

Some states reserve the right to declare an agreement unenforceable if circumstances change drastically. In some states agreements must be "fair and reasonable" when made and not "unconscionable" at the time they are carried out. Needless to say, the terms are difficult to define. As a result more and more agreements are being decided by the courts.

A Texas judge ruled that "in determining whether a contract is unconscionable or not, the court must look to the entire atmosphere in which the agreement was made, the alternatives, if any, which were available to the parties at the time of the making of the contract, the non-bargaining ability of one party, whether the contract is illegal or against public policy and whether the contract is oppressive or unreasonable."[2]

The law does not protect you from signing a bad agreement. As one judge put it, "A party who knowingly has entered into a lawful contract which may be improvident . . . is not entitled to protection from the court(s) which are not free to change his contract for him or to avoid the results thereof."[3] The fact that an agreement may not seem fair doesn't help either—if you signed.

An agreement that violates a child's right to support will not stand up to court scrutiny.

Courts will also take a look at the way the agreement was executed. State laws may vary but there are four basic reasons an agreement can be invalidated: (1) fraud, (2) failure to disclose fully assets, (3) no separate representation (separate lawyer), (4) agreement was signed under physical duress.

Although any and all of these reasons could knock out

an agreement, a Wisconsin court recently found an agreement fair even though the wife didn't have her own lawyer and her husband hadn't disclosed his finances.

In other words, the rules are constantly changing.

A Florida court declared unenforceable an agreement signed when the husband "sprang" it upon the wife the day before a well-planned elaborate wedding was to occur in a large suite at the O'Hare International Airport in Chicago. He pulled the agreement from his pocket when the parties were at the jewelers picking up their wedding rings. Passage had already been booked for a honeymoon cruise to Europe, the wife's trousseau had been purchased, invitations for the large wedding had been sent. The husband had made no mention of the agreement prior to the surprise at the jewelery store. The wife certainly did not have independent counsel of her own choosing. "The only evidence of legal advice is that within twenty-four hours before the wedding, when the husband first presented the antenuptial agreement and she rebelled, she spoke on the telephone to his lawyers."[4]

As for signing your own handwritten agreement, this could be a problem. Steven Spielberg wrote one on a piece of paper without consulting a lawyer. Then he and his wife-to-be, Amy Irving, signed it. The agreement wouldn't hold up in court and Irving received one of the largest divorce settlements in Hollywood, reputed to be close to $100 million.

WHY A WOMAN MIGHT WANT
A PRENUPTIAL AGREEMENT

While the primary purpose of such agreements is still to protect the money of the wealthier spouse, agreements have also become almost mandatory for second marriages, where husband and wife want to keep their finances separate so that their children from a first marriage can inherit their property.

Couples who have been through terrible divorces the first time around may think things will be easier should the second marriage not pan out.

As the nature of marital property continues to expand to include professional degrees, pension funds, and even celebrity goodwill—more couples are drafting agreements that exclude these "assets" from division. Many lawyers report that when both husband and wife are starting marriage and are partners in professional practices they might decide ahead of time that their practices will remain separate and the only marital assets they will divide should there be a divorce would be personal property, their home, and any investments they held jointly.

Prenuptial agreements are also the place for some couples to hammer out potential child custody, child support, and visitation rights.

Sometimes couples who might not have considered a premarital agreement are asked to do so by what lawyers call "interested third parties." When there is family money, a parent or grandparent may put pressure on a daughter or grandson to obtain an agreement—sometimes even threatening to cut off the potential heir who does not want to ask his future bride to sign. Many times, partners in law firms or owners of small businesses now insist that all the partners have agreements to insure that a spouse who is a nonpartner will not be entitled to a chunk of the business as part of a divorce settlement.

Some couples want to use the prenuptial contract as the place to discuss the details of marriage, even going so far as to specify the number of times each week they will have sex. One can imagine a tired old couple in their bedroom, valiantly trying to live up to the obligations of their agreement. The courts are less interested in these personal details and are less likely to care about enforcing them. Premarital agreements serve as a plan for the dissolution of the marriage, not for the conduct of the marriage.

Here are some reasons why a woman might want a prenuptial agreement:

1. She has a lot more money than the man she is planning to marry and wants to keep control of her own money.
2. She is marrying for the second time and wants to protect whatever money she has.
3. She lives in a community property state and does not want to give up half of what she hopes to have.
4. She lives in an equitable distribution state and does not know how the courts might divide her assets should the marriage end in divorce, so she wants to establish her own terms.
5. She hopes it will eliminate problems should the marriage end in divorce.
6. She has children from a previous marriage and wants to be sure the children are protected.

7. She has a family business and doesn't want it to end up with his family.
8. She is a partner in a business and her partners want to be sure control of the business will not pass outside the firm.
9. She is the daughter of wealthy parents or has wealthy grandparents who insist she have such an agreement.

Agreements hit deep psychological nerves. Most lawyers can tell you of agreements that were never signed. One attorney tells of a couple who fought so bitterly that they stormed out of his office, never married, and his client never even paid him.

Prenuptials can imply a lack of trust, a signal that the one who wants the agreement doesn't want to share. If you are marrying a man who sees his money as his source of power, he may want you to sign the agreement so that he will not lose this power.

Women who have money may want agreements to be sure they are not being married because they are rich. The groom-to-be's willingness to sign an agreement may prove to her that he loves her for herself and not for her money.

In the not-so-distant past, especially in common law states, a woman virtually turned over her money to her husband. But now, a woman with her own income and assets has a choice. She can decide how she wants to handle her own money, even if she doesn't have a lot of it. A prenuptial agreement can be the place to iron out some of the financial details before marriage.

Inherited money can also play a role, especially if the money has been inherited by a woman from her father.

A woman may want to keep that inherited money for herself. It may be the only thing she got from her father, who was incapable of giving her anything else.

A woman who saw her own parents fight bitterly over money when they divorced may want an agreement in the hopes of avoiding the kind of acrimony she witnessed.

Premarital agreements are signed before the wedding, at a time when couples are supposed to be most in love. For first marriages, especially, it's hard to think about the marriage ending.

So why do people sign them? A friend of mine, who signed an ultimately disastrous agreement—that is, disastrous for her—says, "I didn't want to show that I wanted anything. I thought it was a matter of principle." So she signed an agreement in which she gave up all rights to income and marital property, an agreement her lawyer advised her not to sign.

Another woman revealed that eight years after she signed an agreement she was still incensed about it. She says, "I will always be angry." But like many women, she didn't want to face the embarrassment of calling off the marriage.

Although the idea is repugnant to many women, I suspect few will react as did the fictional Pauline McAdoo in a recent novel by Dominick Dunne, *An Inconvenient Woman*. The beautiful, impeccably bred Pauline has been asked to sign an agreement by her soon-to-be-husband's lawyer. Instead of signing, Pauline flings an inkwell at the lawyer and storms off to Paris. Frightened of losing her, the groom-to-be fires the lawyer, rushes off to Paris, and presents her with a fabulous diamond engagement ring—and, just to make sure, immediately after the wedding presents her with an incredible van Gogh painting.

CHALLENGING A PRENUPTIAL AGREEMENT

Should you sign an agreement and then want to break it, you will have a hard time. Recently, Tim Peters, former husband of Sallie Bingham, the media heiress, tried to do just that. In the agreement, Mr. Peters waived all claims to alimony. When the couple divorced in 1990, Mr. Peters went to court in Louisville, Kentucky, to try and change the terms. The judge said that Mr. Peters "may now feel he made a bad bargain," but that was not sufficient grounds for revoking the agreement. In fact, the judge added that he thought Mr. Peters had married Miss Bingham "for her money and stayed married to her because of the material benefits that the relationship conferred."[5]

On the other hand, Jacqueline Onassis reportedly reopened negotiations with lawyers after the death of her husband Aristotle, and received more money than the original contract mandated.

If you want to challenge a prenuptial agreement in a state that follows the Uniform Premarital Agreement Act, you must prove that the agreement is not valid. For example, if you want to break an agreement because you say you were forced to sign it, you must be able to prove this to the court.

A Minnesota judge recently overturned a prenuptial agreement that provided that each party's earnings during the marriage were to remain separate property. One attorney drafted the agreement and testified that he advised both parties. During the marriage, all expenses were paid from the earnings of one spouse while the other spouse invested all earnings. The court ruled that not only full and fair disclosure is necessary, but each party must be advised by an independent attorney.[6]

An Alabama judge set aside a recent agreement after the bride testified that "she was presented with the document the evening before the wedding, was unable to contact an attorney, and signed it prior to leaving for church with the understanding it would be rewritten."[7]

If your husband-to-be says, "Oh, just sign it now; I'll change it later," run for the hills. He may leave you more in his will, but men seldom change their agreements.

How to Make the Best Deal

Only you can decide whether you are willing to sign a prenuptial agreement, but should you be asked, there are a few rules of the game that you would be wise to understand. Of course, you can always say no.

1. First of all, be sure you have your own lawyer, even if your husband-to-be is paying for it. (Of course, if you don't have proper counsel, the agreement could be voided at a later date, which may be exactly what you want. If this is the case, you already know the game and probably don't need this chapter.)
2. While agreements may be valid without it in some states, be sure your lawyer asks for and receives as much financial disclosure as possible.

3. If you are worried that there might not be any assets—remember even billionaires like Donald Trump can have financial problems—you might ask for some money to be put in escrow. Or you might ask for a noncancelable life insurance policy in case he dies.

4. Inflation is always a problem, so perhaps your lawyer could suggest a clause that will increase the amount of money you receive by the annual rate of inflation.

5. It's also a good idea to try and set conditions under which the agreement might be renegotiated—perhaps after a certain number of years or after the birth of a child. One woman who asked her husband to sign an agreement gave him 10 percent of her assets each year until he had 50 percent. Remember, if you want to change or revoke the terms of the contract, do it in writing.

6. Sometimes you might ask for up-front money. But the transfer should be made after the wedding. If you get the money before you are married, there would be a hefty gift tax. Once you are married, there is no tax on any money transferred between a husband and wife providing the one getting the money is a United States citizen.

7. If you and your husband are partners in business, you might include a buy-out agreement and a valuation agreement to avoid a messy battle in the event of a divorce. (See Chapter 11 for more about this.)

8. You might build into the agreement payout schedules that take into account tax laws. For example, if you and your husband own a house together and you

will end up with the house, the agreement should include the possible tax on the house should you decide to sell it.

Asking for an agreement can be hard. You have to bring up the realities of money at a time when you are only supposed to be thinking about love.

The late Roy Cohn, who drafted one of the three agreements signed by Donald and Ivana Trump, once told me he advised his clients, usually wealthy men, to resort to a series of white lies. Cohn proposed that Mister X go to his fiancée with the idea of a prenuptial agreement and if she says, "Oh, I'm shocked," Mister X can say, "I trust you completely, but my family won't allow it." Other lawyers suggest that the client put the blame on the lawyer.

While this is a somewhat cute approach that may have worked for some rich older men marrying attractive younger wives (seldom do you see a rich young woman marrying a poor old man), it is probably not an approach that bodes well for the success of the marriage. If you want an agreement because you want to be sure you will continue to have control over your own finances, it is better to say so directly.

One wealthy bride-to-be asked her future husband to sign an agreement. He objected. To avoid a fight, she placed all of her assets in a trust to be able to keep them separate when she married—a complicated legal procedure. Other brides may decide to take the risks that marriage entails rather than pursue the idea of an agreement.

One of the biggest problems with prenuptial agreements is the possibility that circumstances may change. You might sign an agreement that will not be enforced until twenty years later. Predicting your financial conditions that far in advance can be exceedingly difficult. As more and more agreements are being signed more and more case law is evolving that suggests that courts may eventually look at an agreement to see not only if it was fair when it was signed, but also if it is fair when it is enforced.

A recent Ohio decision addresses this issue. In this case a couple signed an agreement that was fair and reasonable at the time of the signing. After a fourteen-year marriage, the husband's assets had grown to $8 million. His income was $250,000 a year. The couple's standard of living had changed dramatically. The $200-a-month alimony that the wife had agreed to receive for ten years if the marriage ended was "unconscionable" because circumstances had changed. The judge felt this was grounds to set aside the agreement.[8]

The equality of earnings that you counted on might not materialize and you might have signed away your right to alimony. Women who do this should be extremely careful. Despite the gains women have made, men still continue to earn more, even in the same profession. If you don't consider and admit that your income might not keep pace, you could sign a mine-is-mine, yours-is-yours agreement that will be disastrous should something happen to your marriage.

MISTAKES WOMEN WITH MONEY CAN AVOID

There is little hard evidence that men and women behave differently when it comes to signing prenuptial agreements. Men who are asked to sign such agreements by their future wives do not seem any happier about signing than women who are asked to sign. But many lawyers have anecdotal evidence that women, especially those who have earned their own money, are making mistakes that they don't think men are as likely to make when it comes to prenuptial agreements.

One common mistake occurs when women want to keep everything for themselves. One woman who was marrying for the second time had inherited several million dollars from her first husband. And she wasn't going to give any of it to number two—she wanted it all to go to her children. She insisted on an agreement whereby both parties waived their rights to the other's assets. Over the years her new husband took over a small company that he built into a business worth several hundred million dollars. They live in great style. To all their friends it is a great marriage. But underneath it all she is seething. Why? Well, it seems she went to her husband and asked him if he would, now that he is so rich, give her a few million dollars so she would have a little more to leave to her children. He has turned her down: an eye for an eye. While there could be a subtle psychological factor at work here, women, says one matrimonial lawyer, "tend to be so concerned about the money they earned that they try to protect it at the expense of a long-term gain."

Another common error women with money make is

that they will not take any risks. When a friend of mine married a few years ago, she now reluctantly admits, she signed an agreement with her husband to buy a large house in the country. The house was to be owned jointly. Each would contribute a certain amount of capital and expenses. You can probably guess the rest. They bought the house at an absolute low in the real estate market. They agreed that if they ever split, he would buy her out. This was just before a major real estate boom. When the split came, the house was worth several million dollars and she had to be satisfied with her original investment, which was a lot less.

Often women err just by getting plain bad advice. My friend Margaret was marrying for the second time. The man was from another state. He seemed ideal. He was a partner in a law firm in another state and appeared to be very prosperous.

Her lawyers advised her not to have a prenuptial agreement. They believed, but never checked, the man had more assets than Margaret and that an agreement would be detrimental to her should the marriage break up.

Her lawyers were wrong. And, when the marriage did break up, it turned out he was broke. In fact, he ended up suing her for some of her money and a lot of the marital property, including the sheets she had actually owned before they married.

Had she asked for an agreement he would have had to disclose his assets, for that is mandatory in New Jersey where the couple lived. Failure to do so invalidates the agreement. So unless the man had absolutely lied—which in itself would have been grounds to invalidate the agreement—my friend would have known the score.

If you are already married and don't have an agreement, there is always the "postnup." This works like the prenuptial agreement but might be more difficult to introduce into the marriage.

There are a variety of reasons for wanting one. A New Jersey lawyer reports preparing an agreement for a long-married couple. The wife thought the husband was taking a business risk she didn't like. She wanted an agreement that would safeguard a certain amount of assets.

You might inherit a great deal of money and want to be sure it won't become marital property.

You and your husband might decide to start a business. A postnuptial agreement could settle ahead of time what would happen in the event of either death or divorce.

Or, you might just be worried about the marriage.

In the end, no agreement will ensure a good marriage, and no agreement will mean that you won't have a messy fight should you divorce. If an agreement is made between unequals, there might always be resentment and anger that could even affect what might otherwise have been a good marriage. If you want an agreement because you think the marriage will not work out, maybe you should think again before marrying.

5.
Coming Apart

At the time of their divorce Gerarda Wilhelmina Schoos Unkel Pommerenke and her husband, Roger, owned a home worth $125,000. When Mrs. Pommerenke was awarded only $7,500 as a divorce settlement she appealed the decision—and lost. Mrs. Pommerenke's practice of sunbathing "topless" in the presence of a male guest who "felt free to be in his 'underwear' or nude in the presence of his host's wife and in the absence of his host" did not influence the judge. Nor did it matter that Mrs. Pommerenke was guilty of adultery. What mattered was the $95,582 that Roger Pommerenke saved before their marriage and used for the down payment. Mr. Pommerenke kept his separate property. The marital property was divided equally. The judge decided the case according to modern divorce law—no more judgments about the good wife or the bad husband.

Welcome to the divorce revolution, a reversal of old rules that was supposed to eliminate the accusations and just divvy up the property. Divorce changed in four ways:

1. The grounds for divorce have changed.
2. Property settlements have changed.
3. Alimony has changed.
4. Child support and child custody have changed.

When I grew up, the kind of behavior exhibited by Mrs. Pommerenke would have been worthy of lurid headlines in the local paper. Adultery was one of the only reasons for a divorce. The others were desertion, alcoholism, and physical abuse; insanity was also a reason for divorce. If a wife was caught cheating, she was usually left with nothing. If it was her husband, he usually paid dearly for his errant ways.

Although a woman was recently prosecuted in Wisconsin for an extramarital affair and several states still consider adultery a punishable crime, moral judgments are increasingly removed from the financial decisions of divorce.

The word *divorce* comes from the Latin *divortium*, which allowed for the dissolution of a marriage by mutual consent. The ancient Romans had pretty well figured out the economics of divorce. If there was a divorce and no adulterous activity the wife could recover her dowry within one year. If the wife was guilty of adultery, the husband got to keep one sixth of the dowry. If the wife had done something less damaging, the husband only kept one eighth of the dowry. If the husband was fooling around, he had to return the dowry immediately. He could hang on to the dowry for six months if he had committed a less serious offense. If, said the Roman law, both parties had been guilty of the big A the law acted as if neither party was guilty—that is, the wife got her dowry back after one year.

By the twelfth century in England, divorce had become an absolute no-no. Ecclesiastic courts controlled divorce. Think of the trouble Henry VIII had when he wanted a divorce. In America where we didn't have church courts, divorce was the domain of the judicial courts or the legislatures. The first divorce in America was granted to Mrs. James Luxford in 1639 by a Massachusetts Bay Colony court. The grounds: bigamy. Contrary to what many believe, divorce was allowed in most of the states with the exception of very Catholic South Carolina. After the Civil War divorce decrees accelerated at a frenzy, one divorce in every sixteen marriages by 1880, and one divorce in every six marriages in the late 1920s.[1] By 1990, almost two thirds of all marriages begun in the preceding fifteen years ended in divorce.

GROUNDS FOR DIVORCE

"Grounds" are reasons for wanting a divorce. Divorce changed dramatically on January 1, 1970, when California passed the first "no-fault" laws and changed centuries of thinking that a marriage could only end if one party had hurt the other party. Today all states have some form of no-fault law.

No-fault divorce eliminated the need for blame. When adultery was the principal grounds for divorce, the husband often staged an "assignation" in order to provide the necessary reason for the courts to dissolve a marriage. George Bernard Shaw, in his play *Getting Married*, depicts a scene in which a couple feign an argument that ends with the husband striking his wife in the presence of a witness so the wife could obtain a divorce on the grounds of physical cruelty.

Divorce reformers who supported no fault believed it would eliminate the need for "corroborated perjury."[2] No fault was meant to be a truth-in-divorce law. Couples could now obtain a divorce by mutual consent without trumped-up grounds. Psychological grounds such as irreconcilable differences and irretrievable breakdown can now be enough to qualify for a divorce.

How do you know if you have irreconcilable differences? In California, the leader in no fault, "The court will not consider evidence as to the existence or nonexistence of the 'irreconcilable differences.' In fact, if one says there are irreconcilable differences and the other says there are not, that dispute, in and of itself, constitutes irreconcilable difference." Although the reform movement's detractors worried that "divorce on demand" would hurt women, other states rapidly followed California in adding no-fault clauses. Thirty-five states grant divorces for irreconcilable differences and irretrievable breakdown, six states allow incompatability, and nine states allow divorce by mutual consent. Georgia offers a choice of thirteen different reasons to abandon a marriage ranging from impotence to drug addiction to physical abuse:

1. Intermarriage by persons within the prohibited degrees of consanguinity and affinity
2. Mental incapacity at the time of the marriage
3. Impotency at the time of marriage
4. Force, menace, duress, or fraud in obtaining the marriage

5. Pregnancy of the wife by a man other than the husband at the time of the marriage, unknown by the husband [Notice that even in the gender neutral language of the law, this does not apply to husbands.]
6. Adultery in either of the parties after marriage
7. Willful and continued desertion by either of the parties for the term of one year
8. The conviction of either party for an offense involving moral turpitude and under which he or she is sentenced to imprisonment in a penal institution for a term of two years or longer
9. Habitual intoxication
10. Cruel treatment which shall consist of the willful infliction of pain, bodily or mental, upon the complaining party, such as reasonably justifies apprehension of danger to life, limb or health
11. Incurable mental illness
12. Habitual drug addiction
13. The marriage is irretrievably broken

In other words anyone can get a divorce. New York is one of the few states where, if a couple do not agree to a divorce, the one who wants the divorce must have "grounds" and be able to prove those grounds. In New York State either side can ask for a jury trial for a divorce.

Some states will grant a divorce if a couple have lived apart for a given number of years (Idaho, five years; Louisiana and Maryland, one year; Arkansas, Pennsylvania, Rhode Island, Tennessee, and Texas, three years) even if one party does not want the divorce.

If you cannot get a divorce in one state, you can move to a state with more lenient grounds. You would have to live in that state long enough to satisfy a residency requirement before you could seek a divorce. Your husband can do the same thing. You will get the divorce but you will be subject to the property settlement laws of the state where you lived. Nevada's six-week residency requirement has helped make it the divorce capital of America. Grounds for divorce in Nevada are either incompatability or living apart without cohabitation for one year. If you want sunshine, the Virgin Islands also has a six-week residency requirement.

If you want the divorce—and more and more women do—you can leave the marriage just as easily as your husband.

Some couples, for religious or other reasons, do not want to live together but do not want a divorce. They can agree to a legal separation. This is a formal document that sets out the rights and obligations such as support and child-custody arrangements the couple have with each other. If you have a legal separation, you cannot remarry.

Who Gets What?

While no-fault divorce made the actual dissolution of the marriage easy, some of the old "fault" concepts lingered when it came to the division of marital property. Some states still cling to the idea that the good wife or husband should be better rewarded than the bad. But even in those states where "fault" counts, the fault has to be really egregious to have an impact on the bottom line. Adultery may not be enough these days.

Eliminating marital fault from divorce did not eliminate fights between divorcing couples. With property at stake, divorcing couples began to battle over the value of property, ownership of property, and even what constituted property.

When it comes to divorce, there are several kinds of property. Yours, his, and ours. Lawyers refer to it as marital (ours) and separate (yours or his) property. Some states consider only marital property in divorce settlements. Other states look at all property without making a distinction between marital and separate property for divorce settlements. They are Alaska, Connecticut, Florida, Hawaii, Indiana, Iowa, Kansas, Massachusetts, Michigan, Montana, New Hampshire, North Dakota, Ohio, Oregon, South Dakota, Utah, Vermont, and Wyoming.

Some states exclude inherited property, gifts made to just one party, and income received from disability payments when dividing property in a divorce. Some states have quasi-marital property. This can be a real problem. Property can start out as separate property; for example, your house may have been purchased with money that you had before your marriage. But then your husband, by making repairs or helping with the upkeep, gradually may have transformed it into marital property.

Far more sweeping than the change toward easier divorce has been the change in the economics of divorce. A new concept of dividing marital property at the end of a marriage developed: equitable distribution. The common law states also began to move toward a concept of shared marital property. Before the laws changed, whoever held title to property—usually the husband—owned the property, even if his wife's money paid for it. The only property that the court could distribute in a divorce settlement was property jointly owned by the couple. Equitable distribution was an attempt to redress that situation in the states that do not have community property laws. Equitable distribution laws recognize for the first time the contribution of the housewife to the marriage and frequently to her husband's career. The new law proclaims marriage as an economic partnership, wiping out hundreds of years of dependency. Husband and wife are economic partners, regardless of which partner earned the money. Between 1970 and 1985 all states added some form of equitable or equal distribution of marital property upon divorce.

The old laws protected the state. The state did not want a man to walk out on his wife and children, leaving the state to support them. Sexist, gender-based rules, which were also written to protect the wife, have been abolished. The change in the law came as a result of changes in society. Women are working and can support themselves. Women are no longer seen as dependents. As more women have jobs and are protected by Social Security, medicaid, and unemployment insurance there is less incentive to keep the marriage together. If it ends in divorce, each partner has a right to an equitable, but not necessarily equal, share of the fruits of that marriage.

Equitable distribution was even introduced into some community property states as a means of distributing marital property in a divorce. The meaning of this idea can best be understood by looking at the actual law, as written into the New York State domestic relations law. Marital property shall be distributed equitably between the parties, considering the circumstances of the case and of the respective parties. The law lists the areas the judge must consider:

1. The income and property of each party at the time of marriage and at the time of the commencement of the action
2. The duration of the marriage and the age and health of both parties
3. The need of a custodial parent to occupy or own the marital residence and to use or own its household effects
4. The loss of inheritance and pension rights upon dissolution of the marriage as of the date of dissolution
5. Any award of maintenance under subdivision six of this part
6. Any equitable claim to, interest in, or direct or indirect contribution made to the acquisition of such marital property by the party not having title, including joint efforts or expenditures and contributions and services as a spouse, parent, wage earner, and homemaker, and to the career or career potential of the other party
7. The liquid or nonliquid character of all marital property
8. The probable future financial circumstances of each party
9. The impossibility or difficulty of evaluating any component asset or any interest in a business, corporation, or profession, and the economic desirability of retaining such asset or interest intact and free from any claim or interference by the other party

10. Tax consequences to each party
11. The wasteful dissipation of assets by either spouse
12. Any transfer or encumbrance made in contemplation of a matrimonial action without a fair consideration
13. Any other factor the court shall expressly find to be just and proper

Number 6, or its equivalent in other state codes, quickly became known as "the housewife's contribution." Modern divorce is about dividing assets, regardless of who earned the money and who holds title to the property. Although monetary contributions are important many state laws now mandate that nonmonetary contributions of a wife who stayed home and cared for the family be considered too.

Of course the new laws are written in the newspeak of the late twentieth century, the gender neutral. As one New Jersey judge explained it, "The common law must adapt to the progress of women in achieving economic equality and to the mutual sharing of all obligations by husbands and wives."[3]

The equitable distribution law and other laws gave the wife who stayed at home a claim on marital assets based on her contribution. Two different terms are designated: direct contribution and spousal contribution.

Direct contribution is fairly straightforward. If your husband owned a business before you married him and you worked in the business during the marriage, you made a direct contribution.

Spousal contribution basically says that if you were the wife who stayed at home and baked the bread, you were entitled to some of the marital dough.

Today, only a few state divorce laws omit the value of the housewife's contribution. They are Alabama, Hawaii, Idaho, Louisiana, Michigan, Nevada, New Hampshire, New Jersey, New Mexico, Oklahoma, South Carolina, Texas, Utah, Washington, and Wyoming.[4]

But equitable distribution did not solve some of the problems that its proponents believed it would. Equitable distribution laws only vaguely guided judges. What was equitable? Was it 50 percent of the assets to each, was it 64 percent? Without specific guidelines, equity was at the discretion of the judge.

To further complicate matters, there was a problem as to what even constituted property. Some things were obvious—the marital home, stocks and bonds, cash in the bank, and the family car. A business and the family silver were all fairly tangible assets. But other assets were less clear. What about a pension fund that would have a future value? Equitable distribution set into motion fights over the very nature of what constituted property.

As the divorce revolution has proceeded, the concept of marital property has expanded to include future earnings such as commissions on an insurance policy sold during the marriage, pension plans and other fringe benefits, and stock options. Intangibles such as professional goodwill and professional degrees are frequently defined as marital property.

Celebrity goodwill is another "intangible" that has been included in the division of marital assets. It is a problem most of us won't have. In 1988, the actress and model Marisa Berenson and her husband, Richard Golub, divorced. Golub claimed that the increased value of Ms. Berenson's career during the marriage was marital property and Golub was entitled to some of the proceeds. In a 1988 decision, the courts agreed with Golub that Ms. Berenson's celebrity status was indeed "marital property," although he was not awarded any money.

Consider the story of Loretta O'Brien. When she married in 1974 she was a teacher. Her husband was starting medical school. He received his medical degree almost ten years later. Two months after that he filed for divorce. In a landmark decision that may make Mrs. O'Brien the Rosa Parks of the matrimonial world, she demanded an interest in that license. The reasoning was simple: Even though the license didn't appear to be marital property, the license gave Dr. O'Brien a passport to future earnings. Mrs. O'Brien, who had supported her husband during those early years, would have none of those future earnings unless the license was deemed to be marital property. The New York Court of Appeals agreed with Mrs. O'Brien. She was awarded 40 percent of the value of his license.

Some states consider the professional degree property for the purposes of property division but not alimony. Some states have laws that mandate a division, and some states have case law without definite instructions. Some states are using the value of the degree as a substitute for alimony. An example is the case of a $100,000 award to a wife in Iowa based on her doctor husband's future earnings.

In some states the professional practice is also looked upon as an asset. In Oklahoma, the court considered the increase in value of the husband's practice during the marriage, even though the husband had been in practice before the marriage.[5] The trend would appear to be that the wife who helped her husband earn a professional degree is entitled to some compensation for this. Some states are calling for "equitable reimbursement"—that is, giving back the money that was actually spent. (A good reason to keep accurate records.) But a Pennsylvania judge concluded that the wife was not entitled to be reimbursed for supporting her husband while he was in chiropractic school because she was legally required to support him.

Possibly the largest asset for most couples, besides the family home, is the husband's pension. Many states now treat pensions as marital property subject to equitable distribution. While many women have pensions, most do not. Or if they do, because they tend to leave jobs to have children the value of the wife's pension is generally much less than her husband's.

In New York, pension plans are considered marital property subject to equitable distribution, but recently in Nebraska the court did not consider the husband's pension plan as part of the marital assets. Even in states where a wife can share her husband's pension, she only shares that part of the pension that was earned during the marriage.

Gradually, some states are also beginning to look at the standard of living during marriage when making awards, and not just giving the wife of a long-term marriage a subsistence payment. Sandra Goldman is a good example. She was forty-six when, after a twenty-year marriage, she and her husband, Peter, a neurosurgeon, divorced in 1987. The Goldmans have two children, Wendy and Gregory. Mrs. Goldman, a nurse, did not work during the marriage. Peter Goldman earned $478,560 in 1986. From time to time he receives bonuses and his corporate checking account pays for various personal expenses. He has a large pension fund into which his corporation has paid over $200,000 over the previous three years. The judge awarded Mrs. Goldman $1,000 per week for eight years, $700 alimony and $300 child support, and suggested that she brush up on her nursing skills. Said the judge, "Mrs. Sandra Goldman's opportunity for future acquisition of capital assets and income certainly will never approach that of Dr. Goldman. However, she has an opportunity to be gainfully employed and to invest wisely the distribution of assets pursuant to this judgment."[6] Oh yes, Mrs. Goldman was given the family home and its furniture, with the exception of her husband's guns and a gun cabinet, animal trophies, an elephant-foot fireplace fender, shotgun-shell loading equipment, gun cases, and daughter Wendy's Raggedy Ann doll. She was also given a lump-sum payment of $216,000, payable over five years.

Mrs. Goldman's lawyers appealed the decision. In the appeals court the judges said Mrs. Goldman's award should have been based on the standard of living she and her husband had during the marriage, thus expanding the interpretation of the Massachusetts divorce laws. When the case was retried, Mrs. Goldman was awarded lifetime alimony of $65,000 a year and most of her court fees.

ALIMONY? DON'T COUNT ON IT

There is no question that many women, and a few men, who did not previously have title to property have benefited from the new property laws. But what happens when there is little property to divide? After property division, alimony looms as a major divorce problem. The concept of alimony has changed dramatically. Once again eliminating any distinction between husband and wife, the new statutes were enacted to eliminate the idea of the dependent wife getting a dole from her husband until she remarried, he died, or she committed some act, such as living with another man, that would deprive her of her stipend.

Alimony is awarded in only 15 percent of divorces these days. With or without fault, alimony is going the way of the dinosaur. The trend, say many lawyers, is for women to be self-supporting. Instead of the "permanent" alimony that used to be granted until a wife either died or remarried, alimony today, except in long-term marriages, if it is awarded at all is generally temporary. Lawyers frequently advise women who are contemplating a divorce to hang on for at least the ten-year mark, because that seems to be the magic number for "long-term" marriage, when alimony awards are considered. It is also the number of years you must be married in order to share in your husband's Social Security if you did not work long enough to qualify on your own.

The idea of alimony has changed, and so have the varieties. First of all, there is *rehabilitative alimony,* as if you, the wife, had just had a traumatic accident. This is generally defined as alimony that is given to a wife so that she will be able to learn a skill in order to be able to support herself. The problem here is that, most of the time, women who stayed home did so in order to take care of the children. Now you will be expected to continue to take care of the children while you learn how to support yourself—a good trick if you can do it.

Remunerative alimony is defined as alimony given to

compensate the wife for money spent during the marriage—especially in cases where the wife supported her husband while he earned an advanced degree. Naturally, if your husband supported you while you earned a degree, he is entitled to the same kind of remunerative alimony.

Permanent alimony is the old-fashioned type of alimony.

Lump-sum alimony may also be awarded. This is an amount that is based on the wife's future support requirements and loss of the wife's right of inheriting any part of her husband's estate. Wealthy women have also had to pay lump-sum alimony.

In California, where alimony is called "spousal support," there is a rough rule of thumb that alimony will last for half of the length of the marriage. In that state each county has support-guideline schedules. Here is a sample from one of them:

If the net earnings of one spouse are $300 to $600 per week, maximum support to the other spouse is one third of that income.

If the net earnings of one spouse are over $600 per week, maximum support to the other spouse shall not exceed 40 percent of that amount.

If there is both spousal and child support, the combined amount should not exceed 50 percent of the supporting spouse's net income.

No spousal support shall be provided to any spouse who, following dissolution, has income sufficient to maintain his or her standard of living.

Several state divorce laws eliminate alimony if there is fault. They are Georgia, Louisiana, North Carolina, Virginia, and Puerto Rico.

Then there are the states where you can get alimony, but fault counts against you. They are Alabama, Connecticut, Florida, Kentucky, Michigan, Missouri, Nevada, New Hampshire, North Dakota, Pennsylvania, Rhode Island, South Carolina, South Dakota, Tennessee, West Virginia, Wyoming, and Washington, D.C.

The payment of alimony and the distribution of assets assumes that couples have accumulated some assets during their marriage. Frequently, that is not the case; instead, they may have piled up the debts. In the latter case, divorce settlements become a question of dividing the debts. As the number of people filing for personal bankruptcy has increased, the impact of bankruptcy on divorce has come under more and more scrutiny. According to federal bankruptcy laws, alimony and child support awards are not wiped out by filing for bankruptcy. One bankruptcy question that has not been settled is whether creditors can confiscate property that might otherwise be used for alimony payments.

A big problem with alimony (and child support) can be collecting it. In California, a woman can get an "order of security." This means she can ask the court to order that her husband post a portion of his money for future support. If he does not pay support she can also get a lien placed on any property her husband owns in California so that if he tries to sell the property, the court won't let him transfer title.

In other states you might be able to get an alimony trust. Such a trust pays income to the wife assuring that her husband cannot squander the money. The remainder of the trust either reverts to the husband or to the children of the couple.

Would a woman fare better under the old system or is she better off today? Today the law assumes that a woman can go out and work. So women are more likely to be awarded the new "maintenance" rather than the old lifetime alimony. A lot depends on your earnings capacity. To illustrate this, look what happened in a recent case in Oregon: "Jane Doe," an Oregon housewife whose eighteen-year marriage ended, was awarded payments by her husband of $1,000 per month for two years, $800 per month for six years following that, and $500 for the next sixty-nine months. When Mrs. Doe earned a teacher's license, the judge slashed her alimony by almost 25 percent: $1,000 per month for two years, $700 per month for four years, and $500 for four years.[7]

CHILD CUSTODY AND SUPPORT

No-fault divorce laws and equitable distribution challenged old assumptions about marriage. The new reform mood supposedly reflecting a change in society undermined centuries-old ideas about the need to preserve marriage and protect the family. But an even greater assumption was challenged with a series of new laws about child custody and child support (see Chapter 9).

In the past, a father had the responsibility for supporting his children; a mother was considered responsible for taking care of her children. So when a marriage dissolved, the mother was awarded custody and the father was ordered to pay child support and given visitation rights to his children. The new laws stress equity: Both mother and father had to support the children. And in an even greater break with tradition, fathers could have custody of their children, either joint physical custody, or joint legal custody. What this meant to some was that the best interests of the child should be considered. In some cases, courts were able to decide that the best interests of the child were served when the mother had custody part of the time and the father the other part, including arrangements that left parents driving their children back and forth to each other's houses on a weekly basis.

If joint custody is a possibility be sure you understand exactly what is meant both in your state and by your husband. In a further break with tradition, a Missouri judge recently told a woman that staying at home to care for her children was no longer an option. She had as much of an obligation to work as did her husband.

Were women better off before no-fault and equitable distribution? Probably not. The idea that women were taken care of by alimony prior to the change in divorce laws may be a myth. Critics of what some called divorce on demand cited as evidence statistics showing women plunged into poverty following the no-fault divorce laws. But these figures have since been challenged. Women's lower earnings are not only the result of divorce, but also the generally lower standing of women in the labor market.[8] There is plenty of evidence that the old divorce days weren't so great either. Very few divorced women received any alimony under the old fault system. When they did, judges and ex-husbands used the doling out of alimony as a way to control the wife's behavior after a divorce. And, in those days, fault could be liberally defined. In one case, a fault—read "no alimony"—divorce was granted to a husband whose wife's "preoccupation with social and club activities and failure to prepare [her] husband's meals" constituted marital cruelty. If a woman was at "fault" she didn't get any alimony at all. A woman who was awarded "permanent" alimony could have that money terminated or reduced, if her former husband remarried, because "the support obligations to his new spouse were more important than the claims of a former spouse."[9]

6.

If You Thought Marriage Was Bad, Wait Until You Try Divorce

In theory, divorce reform was supposed to liberate women and end the lying that previously surrounded it. Instead, the new divorce laws have sent women into battle on foot while their husbands have clobbered them from armored cars.

First, let's look at what divorce reform, that means no-fault divorce and equitable distribution of property, was meant to achieve. Guilt about divorce was to be eliminated, bitter fights were to end, and women would no longer be treated paternalistically, but would take their place as equals in the new economic partnership of marriage.

AND THEY DID NOT LIVE HAPPILY EVER AFTER

Instead of the promised equities, there have been increased inequities. Experts who promulgated the new laws are now taking a look at what they have brought about. Articles have begun to appear in learned journals about the unforeseen consequences of divorce reform.[1]

Most women who have been through a divorce in the last ten years don't need a sociologist to tell them the new system is fraught with problems and that women have been the biggest victims.

Sandra Goldman, about whom I talked in the last chapter, is typical. The court proceedings in her divorce took over three years. Her lawyer, Peter Roth, believes there are several reasons Mrs. Goldman had problems.[2] One of her biggest problems was the lack of funds to adequately pursue her case. In Massachusetts, courts are reluctant to issue expert fee costs. These are fees paid to expert witnesses. Expert witnesses who testify as to the value of property usually must be paid at the time they give their opinions. A 1989 study of the Massachusetts court system revealed that judges rarely award expert witness fees.[3] Basically this cuts off a woman's chance to get what she needs, since many times it is the husband who has the information.

Sandra Goldman's plight revealed another inequity. Mrs. Goldman, who had not worked in years, was expected to retrain herself when she was in her fifties in order to work as a nurse. What many women have suspected is finally being acknowledged: "Judges devalue long-term homemakers' contributions to their families and make unrealistic assumptions about older women's opportunities in the paid work force. Thus, dissolution awards give women small shares of marital property and scant short-term alimony, leaving them in extremis financially while their ex-husbands enjoy their former, or even a more comfortable, standard of living."[4]

Another problem was that Mrs. Goldman didn't know about her husband's investments and had no idea of their value. Sandra Goldman's husband controlled the valuation of his assets. As one example, he invested $180,000 and then said it was worth only half. The court accepted his value. Frequently, with privately held stock, only insiders really know the valuation.

The problem, says one lawyer, is that today's fifty-year-old woman looks like what the judge thinks forty should look. She looks like she can go out and work. So that's what the judge is telling her. Women who stayed home and did not build their own careers have lost those years and are not duly compensated.

While housewives have lost out when it comes to splitting assets under the new rules of equitable distribution and no-fault divorce, many high-powered career women also discover that they have made mistakes that subsequently hurt them. Part of the problem is that the very laws that gave the nonworking wife a shot at the marital assets can now be applied to penalize the hardworking woman. Unthinkable as the notion would have been to our grandfathers, men are now demanding—and getting—support from and shares in the businesses of their wives. Lawyers who have dealt with the other side of the coin report that career women are often no more worldly when it comes to protecting themselves than their stay-at-home sisters.

It isn't only the stay-at-home wife who finds she has problems. Jane Smith, an office manager for a medical doctor, noticed one day a telephone call charge from Florida when her husband was supposed to be in Texas on a business trip. Other odd things happened but Jane ignored the signals. She couldn't believe anything was wrong with her twenty-year marriage. Jane's husband, a computer expert, managed everything. He even sold their house before Jane knew the marriage was in trouble. The house was in his name. In a common law state that meant he could use the money as he pleased. He spent much of it on his new girlfriend. When they divorced, Jane was left with furniture she had before the marriage, a trust for her son's education, and bitter memories. Her ignorance cost her dearly.

Jane's story underscores one of the biggest problems for women when their marriages end in divorce. For, while the law stipulates an equitable, or even an equal distribution of the assets accrued during the marriage, often women, especially in common law states, have no access to the marital assets before the divorce. A husband who wants to keep control of the purse strings can simply do so. If divorce occurs, finding out about the assets could be a problem, necessitating the long process of "discovery."

Discovery costs money. In addition, many women simply do not have adequate funds to even hire a lawyer. The funds are controlled by their husbands. So, despite the laws that declare marriage an economic partnership when the marriage is ending, a wife may find it hard to put her hands on any ready cash.

Instead of lying about fictitious romances in order to obtain divorces, some men now routinely understate the value of their investments. The 1989 Massachusetts study reported that lawyers who were surveyed said that only 35 percent of the financial statements filed by men were accurate. The survey reported that "the courts do not take discovery seriously. Discovery requests are often ignored by opposing counsel, and the courts do not enforce them as they do in other, nonfamily litigation."

Even community property states do not solve that problem of control of assets or access to funds for legal fees. And a recent decision in California has taken away one of the few means women in California had to raise money to finance their divorces. Since California is a community property state, each spouse is considered owner of half the marital property. So women were able to obtain funds by signing promissory notes for their half of the house. When a husband brought suit recently against the lawyer who accepted his wife's promissory note, the California supreme court declared the transaction void, thus eliminating a potential source of funds.

Sometimes, even a savvy wife does not get her fair share of the assets. While each divorce is a separate consideration, a pattern has emerged that to some degree is consistent. In court decisions, distribution of assets has been one third to the lower wage earner and two thirds to the higher wage earner. The wife, who stayed home with children in a long marriage, may receive 50 percent of the property, seldom more. In Texas, which has no alimony, a nonworking wife may receive more than 50 percent of the assets to offset the lack of alimony. But what happens when there are no marital assets?

If you worked with your husband to build a business, do not assume that it is equally yours and his unless you can prove it. Show that your money was used or keep track of the hours you worked. Be listed as a partner or an executive. When famed realtor Donald Trump announced that his wife, Ivana, would become president of New York's Plaza Hotel, Mr. Trump announced that her salary would be $1 a year plus all the dresses she could buy. While that may have sounded cute, Mrs. Trump would have been better off asking for stock.

When my friend Rhoda married her husband, a struggling artist, Rhoda was earning $50,000 a year. Her husband was a free-lance graphics designer. Pretty soon, however, he decided to open his own design firm. Rhoda helped finance it. She also took care of the books. They pooled their income. But that was all they pooled. Rhoda also did all the housework, while her husband began to play house with a beautiful architect who came in to order business cards. I'll skip all the details about Rhoda's attempt to ride out the affair and get right to the point. When Rhoda's husband finally left her, Rhoda lost her job and her husband had shut down his business in order to start a new one with his new companion. Rhoda is sure her husband diverted some cash from the old business to the new one but she can't prove a thing.

It is not unusual for a man to start a business with the help of his wife, who may use her earnings to support the household or may otherwise enable her husband to get started. When the marriage dissolves, it's usually the man who keeps the business.

The new laws do not make alimony a prime focus. There are 17 million divorced women in America. Only 15 percent receive alimony. In the past, alimony was all women really got no matter how long the marriage—property settlements were not part of the package. The premise of the new laws was that women didn't need alimony. They could leave a marriage and go out to work. When *Satanic Verses* author Salman Rushdie filed for divorce, his wife, Marianne Wiggins, declared that she didn't believe in alimony. In New Jersey one judge saw women as "lusting" after a permanent meal ticket. Feminists declared their opposition to the idea of being supported by former husbands. That was fine for the working woman. But it wasn't so great for the woman who had stayed home to take care of the children and had given up her career to help her husband. In cases where there is substantial property, alimony is important but not critical. Alimony is awarded less and less. In some states, there is no chance for alimony, only property division. So, if you and your husband spent all your money and didn't build any assets, there will be little to divide. Unless you can support yourself, you could have a difficult time.

The family home, which used to be automatically awarded to the wife, is now sometimes sold, and the proceeds are split. If there is an income-producing business it frequently goes to the husband. The wife might be given a lump-sum payment. While the initial division was equal, over time the wife loses out.

If the woman wants to keep the home, it could be equally disastrous. For example, if you live in California and your one asset is a house worth $200,000, in order to keep that house, you would have to come up with some way to give your husband his share of the money. You may end up bargaining away other things to keep the house, only to discover that you can't afford to maintain it. Or you may accept an appraised value of the house that turns out to be too high. When you try and sell the house, you will discover that you have lost money. You may accept the house and then discover, when you finally sell it, that you must pay a big tax because the house has risen in value. Chances are, that tax payment was not figured into your settlement.

And the worst of all catastrophes for most women now looms as a possibility. Equal rights language built into our laws suggests that a father has as much right to custody as a mother. Fear of losing her children has been added to the problems of divorce. While some men genuinely want custody of their children, lawyers across the country report that most men will use custody as a negotiating tool. They will threaten to seek custody of the children, then will agree to drop their demand for custody if the wife agrees to take a smaller property settlement or less alimony than she thought she deserved.

Matrimonial lawyers give several reasons why women do not end up with the stake they should after a divorce.

WHY WOMEN LOSE OUT

1. Women do not have records of the family finances before the divorce. When a divorce looms, they discover that "our" accountant has become "his" accountant.
2. Women do not know the value of the assets.
3. Women do not have the money to hire the experts to locate and value the assets during a divorce.
4. Women do not have the money to support themselves during the divorce process if their husbands refuse to send money, so they settle for less than they should.
5. Women do not have the money to pay for lawyers.

The reasons all add up to the same thing: a lack of financial equality at the bargaining table.

For some women, a divorce is their first experience with lawyers and negotiations. They may be married to men who are routinely involved with contracts, closings, and other details of business. For such women, the whole process of divorce can be more traumatic than for their husbands. Unfamiliarity with the process could also be a reason for settling for less.

The new laws have done little to reduce the acrimony of divorce. While divorce fights center around money and property, the fights manifest the emotional problems of the marriage. One couple fought bitterly in court about whether three African violets were marital or separate property. They were not fighting about money—the plants weren't even rare. They were fighting about control and winning, probably the same fights they had during their marriage.

Divorce is hell, no question. It's hell if you are Jane Doe or Jane Fonda with her looks, her fame, and her money. Fonda, who was divorced from her second husband after a seventeen-year marriage, described the process as "debilitating and frightening."

The same women who were dominated financially during their marriages allow themselves to be dominated in the divorce. They even hire lawyers who take on the role their husbands did, letting their lawyers make decisions for them. One woman, terrified of being alone, realized that she allowed her husband to talk her into giving up money by suggesting a reconciliation, which he never meant.

Should you be headed for a divorce, a compromising picture of your husband with another woman will not be nearly as important as a picture of his financial statement.

Some people who want a divorce begin making plans to bail out long before D day. Men have deferred bonuses or even postponed new positions until after a divorce in order to lessen the amount of money they might have to pay their wives. One trick for small business owners and professionals is to prepay expenses, while deferring income. Women who are contemplating a divorce are advised to stock up on groceries while their husbands are still paying the bills and to stash away cash. And while strategies for bailing out of a marriage are usually financial, one woman found her husband's "battle plan" in his briefcase. It called for him to begin bodybuilding to improve his pectorals in preparation for life with a younger woman.

If you already know about the family finances, you are way ahead of many women, especially those who are taken by surprise when their husbands want a divorce. Matrimonial lawyers suggest that if divorce is at all a possibility, you begin your preparations by ferreting out financial information. Of course, you are better off if you have been participating in the financial decisions of your marriage all along. You will need this information if you actually do get a divorce. If you don't get the divorce, having the information will still be helpful to you and beneficial to your marriage.

The hardest part of divorce, many women report, is making the decision that the marriage is over. How do you know when to even call a lawyer? There are several different situations, and each requires some thought. If you think the marriage is in trouble but are not sure you want a divorce, you should do the following:

1. Visit a therapist or marriage counselor. If you and your husband are able to discuss the problem, you can go together.

2. Begin gathering together all of the financial information you need if you haven't already done it.
3. Consult a lawyer. Don't worry that consulting a lawyer will lead you down the road to divorce. If you don't consult a lawyer, your husband may begin making secret divorce preparations and you will lose out.

If you think, as many women do, that your husband would never do anything underhanded, think again and pick up the phone. You don't have to commit yourself to a divorce. You can make perfectly clear the exploratory nature of your visit. The worst thing you can do is ignore the situation thinking that your husband would never do anything to hurt you. Believe me, he could. And you may find yourself doing things you never thought you could.

If your husband walks in one day, as happened to one woman shortly after she returned from a trip, and announces that he is leaving you, immediately proceed to step three. Your husband has already hired his lawyer.

If you have made up your mind that you want the divorce, you may only need steps two and three.

If you and your husband have agreed to a divorce, you may be able to choose less adversarial divorce methods.

If you heard about a vaccine for a disease that was bound to strike one out of three people, you would probably dash for the doctor to get a dose. Yet few of us are willing to take the same precautions about divorce.

If divorce is a possibility, plan carefully.

Divorce Battle Plan

1. Copy all bank records, real estate deeds, credit card statements, and tax returns you can find. This will help establish marital standard of living as well as marital property and debts (see step eight).
2. Some experts will advise women who have joint accounts to withdraw half the money, especially if there is a chance that you will have a hard time getting living expenses from your husband. It is not illegal for you to withdraw money from a joint account. That's what a joint account means—you both own it jointly. Many women who decide to do this discover that their husbands, having planned the divorce in advance, have already taken the money. Some experts, however, say that doing this can disrupt and exacerbate what otherwise might have been amicable divorce proceedings. Base your actions on your knowledge about how your husband is likely to react.
3. If you do not have credit in your own name, open charge accounts at department stores and with major credit card companies while you are still married. But if you go out on a spending spree with the cards, you could be liable for the debts. If you are just getting married, you do not legally have to change the names on all your charge accounts. You can keep some credit in your own name.
4. If you have children, begin a child-care diary: who feeds the children, who does the laundry, who plays with them. This can be helpful if there is a custody battle.
5. Try and accumulate enough cash for expenses for six months and enough to pay initial legal fees, if possible.

6. Many lawyers advise a woman who can do so to take some courses that will help prepare her for the job market if she is not working or for a better job if she is.

7. If you have stocks, call the broker and find out their value.

8. Be able to document your standard of living. If you and your husband traveled a lot, even though his business paid for it, that is part of your way of life. If you had a car and it was owned by your husband's business, or any other expenses that were paid for by your husband's business, include that information. This also helps in determining the value of your husband's business. He may have been charging expenses to the business that would therefore make the business appear less profitable.

9. Be able to document your "spousal contribution." If you traveled with your husband for his business, be able to explain the business nature of what you did, even if it is something as simple as giving suggestions to your husband when he prepared a speech. Business consultants charge money for things many wives do automatically. If you actually helped keep business records be able to show that too. And this does not apply just to women who are at home. Many highly successful women come home from their own offices to help entertain their husband's business clients. It seldom works the other way, except in TV commercials.

10. Try to establish a list of property that may be your separate property. (Some states—Connecticut and Massachusetts, for example—consider all property for distribution in a divorce.)

11. If you own the business and it was started with a loan from the bank in your name, or with a loan from your uncle Henry, be able to document this.
12. List your outstanding debts. If you have a credit line, find out what property is secured.
13. Some lawyers say that even when fault isn't supposed to count, if it exists, use it. Fault, by the way, doesn't have to mean a picture of your husband with that other woman. It can also mean economic fault. Your husband could have wasted the marital assets. If you can show that he did so, for example, by running up debts to finance a fancy trip for himself, that will be helpful when it comes to dividing the assets because his debts may be counted against his share. In 1988 Mark Gastineau, star New York Jets football player, abruptly retired to spend more time with actress Brigette Nielsen. As a result, Gastineau forfeited half his salary for that year. The judge awarded Mrs. Gastineau one third of the marital assets. He included in Mrs. Gastineau's share of the assets the one-third value of Mr. Gastineau's forfeited salary.[5]

Getting this information beforehand is invaluable. Once the battle lines of divorce are drawn it could be extremely expensive to go through the formal legal process called discovery for information that might be available to you.

If you don't know what's going on, your husband will have an advantage in negotiating a settlement. He will have a better idea of what assets you have and what they are worth. Despite all your initial hopes that your divorce will be different from those messy ones you heard about, you may have to fight dirty too. If you think your husband has been hiding assets you might have to hunt for them.

There are a lot of things you can do on your own. However, some people hire detectives to ferret out hidden funds. If you are feeling squeamish about this, know that you can buy a lot of information for $30 to $50 an hour. Here's a tip, however, for anyone thinking of hiring a professional. Work through your lawyer. If you hire the detective directly, there is no client-attorney privilege; your husband's lawyer can demand discovery and get a court order to look at the files. If your lawyer does the hiring, the detective is accountable only to your side. You wouldn't usually do this unless you were on the point of litigation.

How to Hunt for Hidden Assets

1. If you want to go the do-it-yourself route, you will need to invest in some equipment. A small tape recorder is a must for taping phone conversations. It's legal if you are taping conversations between you and your husband.

2. A prime source of information that is right in your house is the trash basket. Investigate it—you never know what you could find. Possible treasures that could turn up include old checks revealing bank accounts you didn't know about and credit card slips.

3. If your husband goes to the Cayman Islands a lot and he's not an avid fisherman, you could suspect that he has a bank account there.

4. Check the postmarks on the mail. In fact, check all mail.
5. If you find an unfamiliar key, it may be for a safe deposit box. Try and find out.
6. Illegal cash is risky. It is illegal. However, sometimes women use this as a negotiating point. Remember, if you knew about such cash when you signed joint tax returns, you will be in trouble too.
7. Your husband's office could be a treasure trove. If you can get inside long enough, copy as many documents as you can find, especially insurance policies, leases, and bank statements.

There Is More Than One Way Out

Although most of the divorces that hit the newspapers pit one well-known divorce bomber against another, divorces do not have to be like that. There are several routes to divorce.

You can do it yourself. There are several books on the market. Some courts even sell the forms. The do-it-yourself divorce is recommended for couples who have few assets, few debts, and a very brief marriage; where there is no question of child support or alimony; and where you each decided, if you have pension plans, to keep your own.

You can go to a legal clinic. You should be in somewhat the same situation as the do-it-yourself group: short marriage, few assets, no children, and few debts. This is a little more expensive than doing it yourself, but at least you have someone to answer any questions you may ask.

You can go to a mediator. Mediation is the hot buzzword of the divorce profession. As with the do-it-yourself divorce, some people are more suited to it than others. Mediation, or alternative dispute resolution (ADR), as it is also called, is an alternative to the traditional court resolution of disputes. A family mediator is a specially trained independent expert who sits down with a husband and wife and helps them come to an agreement. Many mediators started out as lawyers or therapists. The mediator does not make decisions or give legal advice. Unlike arbitration, where a couple would submit to a binding decision by a third party, a mediator tries to help a couple reach their own agreement. A settlement is not imposed. Mediation can be used to settle the whole divorce or a few sticky issues such as child custody, alimony, or property issues. Some states have court-mandated mediation for child custody and visitation issues.

The laws work differently in every state. For example, in California, parents who seek custody in the court must attempt mediation before taking their case before a judge. In Delaware, all contested custody, visitation, and support cases must be submitted for mediation. The Delaware laws specify a formula for support based on income and other criteria. The Kansas law recommends mediation of issues involving children and encourages the use of mediation in property settlements.

Divorce lawyers do not like mediation. Lawyers say that women are generally at a disadvantage in mediation. Says one, "I have seen women getting nailed in mediation, particularly when they have an imbalance of power with the spouse. I can give you countless examples of women who are married to high-powered, controlling men who push mediation because in the mediation sessions they can continue their intimidation and control where they cannot do that in a litigation setting." If this is true in your marriage, mediation is not for you.

Many lawyers say that mediators who were trained as therapists do not understand the financial complexities of divorce.

Mediation requires the voluntary participation of both husband and wife. If your husband refuses to go to a mediator, you can't go alone.

If you have little knowledge of the family assets, mediation will be a disaster. One couple who chose mediation after a twenty-year marriage were determined to avoid the conflicts they had seen in other divorces. They worked with a mediator to reach an agreement. Throughout their marriage they had always pooled their income, she as a lawyer, he as a stockbroker. During the marriage, money was seldom a problem. They had agreed early on that any money either one would inherit would go directly to their two children.

Their biggest asset was a house that they bought for $75,000. During the real estate boom of the eighties the house became worth $1,800,000. Their other major asset was his pension plan. They had very little in savings. They had some cash. They agreed that they would split everything and she would buy out her husband's share of the apartment. They showed the agreement to a lawyer who wrote the necessary legal documents and took care of the mechanics of the divorce. They decided to take their gross income as a basis for paying a proportionate share of the cost of supporting their two children. Presently, that is one third for her and two thirds for her husband. But the wife is hopeful her income will increase and that she will then pay more of the child support.

Cost for the whole process: $2,000 to the mediator and $500 for the lawyer.

The wife thinks that she might have gotten more money, but she had confidence that she would earn money and she and her husband agreed that they did not want fights about money. Most couples say that, but it doesn't work out that way. Possibly it worked in this case because they both knew exactly what the assets were and both felt confident of their ability to earn money.

If you are thinking about hiring a mediator, be sure the mediator is a member of the American Bar Association or the Academy of Family Mediators. The American Arbitration Association will also recommend mediators; you must pay a fee of $125 for the recommendation.

Divorce Really Hurts

The traditional way of divorcing is to hire a lawyer who guides you through the complicated procedure. Unlike mediation, which tries to bring parties together, traditional court-battle divorce is an adversary procedure: You and your husband have different interests, you and your lawyer have different interests, your husband's lawyer and your lawyer have different interests. Like war, it is treated as a battle to be won. Getting divorced, unlike getting married, is fraught with complex legal questions as well as emotional reactions. Regardless of your economic situation, whether you work, or have children, the questions you have are likely to be similar to those of other women. Divorce is like any other lawsuit: There is a plaintiff and a defendant. If you want the divorce and file the papers, you are the plaintiff, your husband is the defendant.

Temporary Support

It's nice to think that the man you married will, if he has supported you in the past, contribute to your support during the divorce negotiations. Sometimes that doesn't happen. You may have to go to court to force your husband to support you. Every state has its own form of temporary support. In Pennsylvania, for example, temporary support is based on a formula. If there are no children, the wife's income, if she is the lower earner, is subtracted from her husband's income. The difference is then multiplied by 40 percent.

Example:	Income of husband	$54,000
	Income of wife	20,000
	Difference	$34,000
		× .40
	Amount of temporary support	$13,600

The formula changes if there are children. In New York the court will award temporary support for necessaries and child support if a woman is without funds, but it is at the discretion of the court. In California, a wife with no children and no earnings capacity will be given 30 to 35 percent of her husband's take-home pay. If you are the worker, your husband can receive the same. If you have children, that figure climbs to 50 percent.

Sometimes the courts will award temporary support but husbands will not pay. Then you will have to go back to court. Lawyers suggest that this is done to wear down the resistance of the wife, who will then settle for less because she can't manage without anything. If this happens to you, and you borrow money to pay for groceries, keep a careful record of it.

As far as divorce itself, the legal process can take a long time. Many lawyers believe that couples need this emotional time in order to get through a divorce. Some lawyers suggest that there is a typical emotional pattern to a divorce. Couples begin by thinking they will be reasonable. Then, somewhere along the line, the situation turns bitter and angry. This, say many lawyers, is a necessary part of the separation process. Others, critical of the adversarial nature of conventional divorces, believe the sometimes hostile negotiations cause the anger.

One matrimonial lawyer, now turned mediator, explains negotiation. Lawyers for opposing parties play a "game of legal chess" with the object "to get as much as you can and give as little as you have to. The rules are that there are no rules." He believes that frequently lawyers raise clients' expectations because the lawyers are stating initial bargaining positions whereas the clients think they are being given final offers. The wife, thinking she has been given a final figure, becomes infuriated, if not insulted, by the paltry offer made by her husband. The husband, who may be the type who measures his self-esteem by his money, has now been asked to part with a huge chunk of his hard-earned cash. Naturally, his wife's lawyer doesn't think his client will get that figure. The husband is livid. Never, he says. And the fight is on. Sometimes it is only settled when the wife realizes that she cannot afford to play the game anymore because the attorney fees are too high. Sometimes it is only settled when the husband threatens to go to court and his wife suspects that he just might—something she cannot afford.

QUESTIONS TO ASK BEFORE YOU HIRE A DIVORCE LAWYER

Let's assume that you have finally decided that you need a lawyer. Do not walk in and turn your case over to the first lawyer you meet. This is going to be a critical time and it is best to do some research. Get several recommendations from friends or call your local bar association for a list of matrimonial lawyers in your area. Ask if you will be billed for an initial consultation.

1. What type of practice do you have (e.g., matrimonial, corporate, litigation)?
2. Do you usually represent men?
3. What are the costs? Most lawyers will quote an hourly fee, usually between $75 an hour to as high as $350. The problem is, almost no lawyer will be able to estimate the number of hours your case will take.

    Your prospective lawyer will also try to assess you, to figure out how much your case will bring in legal fees. You must realize the longer your case takes, the more money your lawyer can earn. There is a built-in conflict of interest.

    Some lawyers will take a flat fee, but if the case takes much longer than anticipated will probably come to you to ask for more money. Nobody wants to work for nothing, so if you do not ante up more money, you may not be getting the best from your lawyer.

    Some lawyers will charge a percentage of whatever

you receive as your settlement. Be careful if they do; in most states it's illegal. Others may ask for a bonus if the case was settled very quickly and your settlement was substantial.

4. When will I be billed? Billing is extremely important—especially if you do not have much money available because your husband has taken most of it away. While some lawyers may work with you without asking for too much up front, if you need appraisers or experts, they are expensive and must be paid right away.

5. Will my husband pay my fees? Many women assume that their husbands will pay the legal fees and therefore it is not important to worry about the costs of the divorce. Do not make this assumption. Be very careful, even if your husband offers to pay your legal fees. One lawyer, David W. Belin, recalls learning a lesson when he was just starting his practice. His client was a wealthy man. The lawyer representing the wife was a well-known matrimonial lawyer. Belin's senior partner told him to contest every financial demand made by the wife's attorney—except for the fee. That was to be paid. In other words, the wife's lawyer would be willing to settle for less, on behalf of his client, the wife, as long as he knew that his fee would be paid. If at all possible, a wife is better off paying her own fees.[6]

6. Will you require a retainer (money that you give in advance)? Your lawyer then deducts the hourly fee from this until it is used up. Ask to be informed of how much money is being spent along the way.

7. Will you personally handle my case or will I work with one of your assistants?

8. Will I be able to reach you over the weekend (or at all)? This is often a big complaint. Not getting your

lawyer on the telephone can be extremely frustrating. One woman received a call from a neighbor while she was at work. Her husband was moving furniture out of their jointly owned home. As it was jointly owned, there was nothing to be done to stop him. By the time she reached her lawyer, it was too late—the furniture was gone.

9. Will I need to sign a contract? A good idea. Be sure to read it very carefully. It will set out the boundaries of the work your lawyer will do. Be sure to ask about any postdivorce settlement negotiations that may be necessary. One woman found, after she had reached a settlement with her husband, that he refused to turn over the specified property. Her lawyers told her they did not handle any after-divorce proceedings.

10. Will I be given copies of all documents and will you explain their meaning? Much of what goes on is the technical filing of motions. Many women complain that they are not told about this by their lawyers.

But above all, ask yourself, is this someone you will get along with, feel comfortable telling intimate details of your married life? Don't overlook any negative signs. Does your lawyer concentrate on you or constantly interrupt you to answer phone calls?

Are there any ways to minimize the cost of a divorce? Here are some tips from a top New York matrimonial lawyer:

1. Don't use your lawyer as a psychiatrist.
2. Have as much information as possible available.
3. Listen to what your lawyer says.

My own money-saving tip: Anytime you must call a lawyer on the telephone, have a list of questions that you want to ask. Write them down. Then arrange a time to speak with your lawyer. Remember that lawyers usually charge for telephone calls. Most often you will receive a minimum charge of fifteen minutes—whether you speak for five or fifteen the price will be the same. Wait until you have a few questions before you place your call. Keep a large clock nearby to remind you of the cost.

Another money-saving tip: Don't sleep with your lawyer. And if you do, make sure you're not being billed for the time. At least that's what Sherry Kantar, of Chicago, Illinois, claimed happened to her. A trial is pending. Her ex-lawyer says the allegations are "nonsensical."[7]

Above all, you have to help manage your case. You cannot just hire a lawyer and think you are being taken care of by a benevolent mother or father. Remember Rhoda, who didn't keep any records of the money she had put into her husband's business? Well, she made the same mistake when she hired a divorce lawyer.

Rhoda sent the lawyer a $5,000 retainer. Rhoda never saw any bills, never had a breakdown of expenses, and never asked a single question. When the lawyer called and asked for more money, Rhoda was astonished. Then she asked for an accounting and discovered lots of charges for late-night taxis and dinners. Rhoda demanded an explanation; after all, her case hardly required burning the midnight oil. The lawyer agreed, and Rhoda received credit for the taxis and dinners.

But managing your case means more than watching the legal bills. It means being realistic about when to fight and when to give in. One woman reports that she and her husband had agreed on almost everything. Then the lawyers stepped in, and she was too frightened to say anything when the lawyer escalated her original demands. She ended up with about the same settlement she had originally expected, but with much higher legal fees.

Sometimes, whatever you do, you will not end up as well as you would like. One reason may just be the state in which you live.

Here's what I mean. Recently, Amy and her husband decided to divorce after a ten-year marriage. During the marriage they managed to accumulate substantial assets. The trouble is, the assets were mainly his. In nine of the ten years of marriage Amy, a book editor, earned more than her husband, a professor. But during those ten years Amy free-lanced, while her husband taught at a large university. He had a pension plan. While she will share in the value of the plan, her share will be based only on the years during which they were married. She will not be able to continue to share in his plan. Her husband will continue to have his medical insurance, while she will have to find her own plan. True, she will be able to continue her husband's plan for eighteen months, but then she will have to buy her own insurance. But the most galling part of the split is the $150,000 her husband inherited from his uncle. In New York, that money is separate property. She gets none of it. Had they lived in Massachusetts, only a short drive away, that marital property distinction would not be made.

Your lawyers can give you a general idea of the way judges in your state or community are likely to decide various areas of a dispute, should your case go to court. Naturally you would like to avoid that. Once you have hired a lawyer, sit down and talk realistically about your chances.

Important Questions to Ask Your Lawyer

1. What are my state's general rules about property division? For example, in New York property is usually divided with the wife, usually the lower-earning spouse, getting between one third and one half of the marital assets. It will more likely be one half if there has been a long marriage, several children, and a wife who has not worked. In Pennsylvania, you are more likely to get a fifty-fifty split.
2. What happens in my state concerning a professional degree or professional practice? If you supported your husband while he went to medical school, will you be reimbursed for the actual money that was spent or will you be given a share in your husband's future earnings?
3. What are the laws in my state about alimony: lump-sum alimony; rehabilitative alimony (some states have abolished this form of alimony); remunerative alimony; and permanent alimony? (See pages 81–82 for definitions.)
4. How is a pension divided in my state? In some states the pension will be awarded as a lump-sum payout to the wife, immediately. In other states the pension will be awarded when the husband actually receives it. Since pensions are regulated by federal law you need a special document called a qualified domestic relations order (QDRO) to make sure you get what you're supposed to.

5. How is the family home likely to be divided? In some states the courts order the home to be sold and the proceeds to be divided, either in equitable distribution or in community property. Some states allow a wife to stay in the home with the children until the children reach a certain age, and then order the home to be sold. If you are awarded the family home, and there is appreciated value, make sure you know what the taxes will be. In some cases a judge will not make allowances for future taxes. For example, if you and your husband paid $100,000 for your house and you then sell it for $200,000, you will have to pay capital gains tax on the $100,000. If you and your husband split your assets fifty-fifty but you then have to pay taxes on your half, you have come away with a bad deal.

6. What about child support? Some states have a definite formula, frequently requiring support to come from both parents, depending on their ability to pay.

7. Will I be awarded medical insurance for myself or the children? If your husband has medical insurance from his company, you must be allowed to continue that coverage for at least thirty-six months after your divorce.

8. What about alimony trusts? If you have reason to believe your husband will not pay what he is supposed to, ask your lawyer about alimony trusts. Such trusts usually pay income to the wife and the remainder of the trust either reverts to the husband (usually the donor) or to the children of the couple.

9. How does my state consider standard of living? Remember the Goldman case because this is a new area of the law that is not really established. In California

recently, instead of awarding a wife support based on the couple's standard of living, the judge criticized the couple's high living, which he felt had been unrealistically maintained.[8]

10. What are the rules for temporary support in my state?

11. How can I make sure I collect what's due? Collecting can be a problem. If your husband also has title to the assets, even though you are awarded a property settlement you may have trouble collecting. In a 1988 New York divorce, Brenda Ritz was awarded $406,162, which she was to receive over a ten-year period. Three years later, Mrs. Ritz had not collected any of the money.

12. How can I keep my husband from transferring assets? If you have any reason to believe your husband is transferring assets, your lawyer may be able to get an injunction prohibiting your husband from moving the assets out.

WHEN TO SETTLE

A big problem in divorce is knowing when to settle. By the way, 90 percent of divorces do not reach the courts. Those that do, say many lawyers, are sometimes based on unrealistic expectations. Sometimes these expectations can be fueled at an early meeting with your lawyer when he suggests that you should receive a certain settlement. Sometimes they are brought about by a sense of anger or guilt, a feeling of being wronged and therefore wanting what you consider your rights.

The more you understand the financial realities, the more likely you will be to avoid these escalating battles. Often fights develop over an amount of money that, if split, would give each of you more than you will end up giving your lawyers. Yet many couples continue to wage war, ending in a pyrrhic victory for one of them and expanded fees for their lawyers.

If you and your husband are very far apart on what you think you should get, try to estimate what the court expenses might be plus your other legal fees. Then subtract that amount from what you think you are going to get. Then decide again whether you want the emotional strain of a court battle.

The emotional scars that these fights can leave may not be worth the struggle. Studies suggest that women who have been divorced for five years are happier than men who have been divorced for the same amount of time.

While the chances are unlikely that you will find yourself in a divorce court, you should know a few things about that. First of all, court cases are very expensive. The hourly fees that you will have to pay your lawyer will add up. In addition you may have to pay hefty fees to a variety of experts to help prove your point—expert appraisers, if there is a business, experts in stock options if those exist, and a myriad of other experts. In some states you may also have to pay for the costs of the court.

This doesn't mean that you should capitulate on every demand. It just means you don't want to end up like the couple in *The War of the Roses.*

UNDERSTANDING THE BOTTOM LINE

1. If you are offered the house as an offset against other assets, know what taxes you will have to pay when you sell the house. This is true for other assets, such as stocks that you may acquire in a settlement.
2. Decide if you are better off with a lump-sum payment or a steady stream of income over a longer period of time. Ask your lawyer or accountant to help you figure out the differences.
3. Do not be tricked into settling on an amount and then discovering that the money is to be paid out over a long period of time, thereby lessening its actual value. If you do not understand the discounted value of money, you could be hurt. Briefly, this means the $1,000 that you get today is worth more than the $1,000 that you might get in five years. Over those five years the money will lose its purchasing power, depending on the rate of inflation. This is a figure that is easily calculated using a discount table.
4. Do not accept a property settlement that is then paid out over a ten-year period as alimony. There are two reasons not to do this. The first reason is that alimony is taxable to the recipient, so you are getting less than you thought. The second reason is that alimony can end for a variety of reasons—the court could reduce your alimony if you start working, alimony might end if you remarry, your husband could die or lose his money. If you have young children, an insurance policy might be appropriate; your husband pays it and you are the beneficiary.

5. If you have a lot of doubts about your settlement, get a second opinion.

It is unlikely that the laws will or should change. What will happen is more standards will develop in each state. And there may be some modifications. Some equitable distribution states may change the laws to assure a fifty-fifty split of marital property, for example. More states may become like Wisconsin, where a penalty is levied against the spouse who conceals an asset that is then uncovered. What can change, perhaps, is a woman's knowledge of her family assets. More property in joint name might also help women, because then you share more equally in the assets. Women will continue to work and have their own pensions and medical plans. As more women work they will approach divorce more as equals than as dependents. Then perhaps the laws will be truly equitable.

7.

Retirement? For Whom?

"Retirement?" Carol Needham laughed. "We'll never be able to retire," she said. Carol, aged forty-three, and her husband, Peter, aged fifty, have a ten-month-old baby. Carol, a computer programmer, has recently stopped work in order to be with her baby full-time. Peter's salary, as manager of a bookstore, has never been as much as Carol's. Now, as they try to live on Peter's salary and save for son Gregory's education, retirement seems remote, if not impossible.

This is a big change from earlier centuries. In the early Middle Ages, average life expectancy was forty-five years, but for women it was only thirty to forty years. There were few old people.[1] In 1992 there were 45,000 centenarians. Thirty-five thousand were women. Many of them will end up in financial trouble.[2]

Providing for retirement is a modern concept that grew out of the industrial revolution. The English Poor Law Statute of 1601 stated:

The father and grandfather, mother and grandmother, and children of every poor, old, blind, and impotent person, or other person not able to work, being of sufficient ability, shall at their own charges relieve and maintain every such poor person, in that manner, and according to that rate, as by the justices of that county where such sufficient persons dwell, in their sessions shall be assessed.[3]

Wealthy landowners were expected to take care of their peasants. The early idea of aid was of a service nature. You went to a poorhouse or to the old-age home. There was no system of paying money directly to the elderly or the sick. Otto von Bismarck introduced old-age pensions in the 1880s: It was part of his program of state socialism—not as a liberal measure but to forestall democratic socialism. Bismarck thought the ideal retirement age was sixty-five.[4] By coincidence that was the average life expectancy of the German worker.

For Americans life expectancy has far surpassed that of the German worker of 1880. Planning for retirement is an important concern of most couples. The ideal retirement plan would combine income from three sources: Social Security, private pension plans, and savings and investments.

Social Security

Social Security is the retirement plan administered by the federal government, available to all workers who pay Social Security taxes (known as FICA on your paychecks). When you retire your Social Security benefits are determined by the amount of money you have paid into the system and the number of credits you have earned.

The number of credits depends on the number of years you have worked. For most women that is a lower number than for most men. In 1992 women received only 75 percent of the benefits men received.

While Social Security was never intended to provide all of your retirement income it is the only retirement fund for one out of five women over the age of sixty-five. You can begin collecting benefits when you are sixty-two, but you do not get maximum benefits until you are sixty-five. In the year 2000 the retirement age will begin to creep up. Anyone born between 1938 and 1959 will not collect full benefits until age sixty-seven.

Social Security does provide benefits for nonworking wives or husbands. If you are married you can collect a retirement benefit equal to half of your husband's benefits. In other words, if your husband is entitled to $1,022 in monthly benefits when he retires, you would be entitled to receive a monthly benefit of $511. You and your husband would have a combined income of $1533 per month.

If you also worked, you will probably have your own Social Security benefits when you retire. However, you may discover that half of your husband's benefits are more than your own benefits, which are likely to be lower. (You can't get both your own benefits and benefits as a wife, but you can get the higher of the two.) In other words, you lose either your working benefit or your benefits as a spouse.

If your husband dies and you were married at least nine months, you may be entitled to survivor's benefits provided by Social Security. As a widow you would receive the same amount your husband received when he was retired. If you have your own Social Security benefits, you would receive either your own benefit or your survivor benefit; you would not get both. If you and your husband had a combined Social Security income of $1,533 per month—$1,022 for your husband and $511 for you—and your husband died, you would receive his full benefit of $1,022 or your own full benefit if it was higher. If you remarry before age sixty, you lose your widow's benefits, no matter how long you were married. But in the eyes of Social Security, older is more valuable. If you remarry after you reach age sixty, you can continue to receive your widow's benefits and still remarry.

If you are divorced you may also be entitled to benefits based on your former husband's benefits if you were married for at least ten years, are sixty-two or older, and still unmarried. You can collect benefits if you have been divorced for at least two years, even if your ex is still working. But you will get a higher benefit if you can wait to start collecting. If your husband has more than one ex-wife collecting benefits on his account, well, even Uncle Sam draws the line and limits the amount that can be paid on each Social Security record to an amount usually equal to about 150 to 180 percent of an individual's retirement benefits. If there are two exes collecting, you may each get a reduced share.

To find out just what your benefits will be, call the toll free number, 1-800-772-1213, and request a Personal Earnings and Benefit Estimate Statement. Complete and return the form. You will receive back a computer print-out that will give you all of your personal retirement information—past earnings, estimated retirement benefits, disability benefits, and even benefits that may go to your survivors.

PENSION PLANS

"Pension plan" is the umbrella term for a variety of retirement programs that private corporations provide for their employees. The benefits include retirement plans as well as health plans and stock option plans. In 1990 only 40 percent of full-time employees were covered by private pension plans, down from 50 percent in 1979. Only 12 percent of workers in companies with less than ten employees have pension plans.[5] Companies are not required to offer pension plans to their workers. However, those companies that do offer pension plans must comply with federal pension plan rules and in return are entitled to certain tax benefits. Pension plan benefits depend on the number of years you have worked.

Plans come in many varieties, but the premise is always the same: your employer puts money into a separate account where it can be invested and profits can accumulate, tax deferred, while you are working. Therefore, money that is credited to your pension fund is not reported as taxable income on your federal income tax return. You only pay taxes on the money when you retire and begin to take money out of your account. There are two different types of pension plans:

1. *Defined Benefit Plans*—The traditional plans offered by large companies. The benefit you get when you retire is fixed. The company itself contributes to an employee fund. The benefit you get when you retire is based on the number of years you worked, your salary, and your life expectancy. A rough rule of thumb for calculating your defined benefit retirement income

would be 1.5 percent of final pay for each year of service. If you worked for thirty years and your last year's salary was $50,000, your pension would be $22,500 a year. Because the company guarantees a certain payout when you retire, defined benefit plans have become very expensive. Many companies have discontinued them.

2. *Defined Contribution Plans*—The contribution put in, either cash or stock, is fixed, but the amount of benefits you receive at retirement is not; it is based on how well the money is invested. The big advantage to these plans is that your retirement money is growing tax deferred. Defined contribution plans include:

Profit-sharing plans—plans in which the employer's contributions are limited to 15 percent of its payroll with an annual dollar limit per participant of $30,000. The company decides on an annual percentage contribution, and each employee gets the same percentage. Companies are not required to make contributions every year. Don't expect any contributions in a bad year.

Money purchase plans—plans in which the annual contribution is fixed and can be no more than 25 percent of annual compensation. Once a company decides on a percentage to contribute, that amount must be contributed each year.

401(k) plans—plans to which you, the employee, contribute money that is deducted from your salary, thus lowering your income and reducing your taxes. In other words, you finance your own retirement, and the government gives you a tax break. The maximum amount of money that can be contributed each year is fixed. In 1993 the maximum amount was $8,994. Employers may, but do not have to, contribute to your plan. Usually, companies will match employee contributions; for example, if you put in one dollar they will put in twenty-five cents.

ESOPs—plans in which the employer contribution is only company stock.

Pension plans are also available for the self-employed and for employees of small companies. There are various plans called Simplified Employee Pension Plans (SEPs) that employers can establish and to which employees can contribute part of their salary. These are similar to defined contribution and defined benefit plans. There is a limit to the amount of money that can be contributed.

Government and civil service agencies also provide pension plans, usually similar to the 401(k), called the 403(b).

Other plans are available for partners in corporations, even if you are the sole owner. The most popular is the Keogh plan. It is like a 401(k) plan. If you own your own business, you can set up a Keogh plan. If you have employees they must also be allowed to participate in the plan. Your plan must have a sponsor: a bank, a mutual fund, or an insurance company. A professional or trade organization would also be a qualified sponsor.

The plan allows a self-employed person to put in $30,000 or 25 percent of your compensation up to $150,000.

If you have your own company and would like to start a Keogh plan, call the IRS (listed under Department of the Treasury in your telephone book) and request *Retirement Plans for the Self-Employed,* publication 560.

All plans regulated by the federal government must give you a plan summary and a yearly statement. Be sure you study yours and your husband's.

Individuals who work can also start their own personal pension plans, called IRAs (Individual Retirement Accounts). Again, the principal is the same. You put funds into a special account which can then invest while taxes are deferred until you retire or withdraw the funds. IRAs are tricky. You can contribute up to $2,000 per year to an IRA, even if you already have a pension plan at work. You can deduct that money from your federal income taxes, if you are not covered by a pension plan. If you earn over $35,000, you may not take any deduction, although you may still put aside your $2,000 each year.

If you are married and you want to contribute to an IRA, your husband's income is counted as well as your own in determining how much of your contribution is deductible from your federal income taxes. The deductible amount stops when your combined income reaches $50,000 and your husband has a pension plan. A nice little wedding present from Uncle Sam. The working woman, who is not covered by a pension plan where she works, gets hurt the most by this. If a wife works and wants to open an IRA account because her company does not offer a pension plan, she will also be subject to that $40,000 rule. In other words, a wife can lose out on having a tax-deductible pension because of her husband's salary—a salary which may not be there for her, should they divorce.[6] You can contribute to your own IRA and not take the tax deduction. Your money would still accumulate tax deferred, and you would at least have a pension plan. You and your husband should each make your maximum contributions. It's a great way to save. You can probably do it automatically through a monthly accumulation plan at your bank.

How to Have Your Own IRA

If you are not working, you can still have an IRA, called a spousal IRA, really meant for the stay-at-home wife. Here's what you can do. In addition to the $2,000 that your husband can contribute to an IRA, an additional $250 can be contributed to the spousal IRA. But this does not have to be divided $2,000 to your husband, $250 to you. It can be divided in any proportion, as long as neither account receives more than $2,000. Whether this can be tax deducted depends on your husband's income. But, as with an IRA for a working woman, even if you can't get the tax deduction, once you have put the money away, it will increase tax deferred, an important way to build retirement funds.

If you are divorced and receive alimony, you can count that as earned income in order to establish an IRA. But the same income limits apply, so if your alimony is added to your earnings you may have too much income to deduct your IRA. Open one anyway, and let the money accumulate tax deferred.

Typical pension and savings plans might include a defined benefit plan, as well as a 401(k) and maybe some stock options. The defined benefit plan might be invested by the company money managers. For the 401(k) you might be able to choose a group of funds such as a bond fund, a stock fund, and maybe even an international fund.

How to Have Your Own Pension Benefits

1. If you do not work, open a spousal IRA. Your husband can contribute up to $2,250, divided any way you choose, although no more than $2,000 can be contributed to one IRA. If your husband contributes $1,000 to his IRA, he can contribute $1,250 to your IRA. If you are working and you or your husband are already covered by a plan, you can take a full deduction for your contribution, if your combined income is less than $40,000. You get a partial deduction until your earnings reach $50,000. If you and your husband are not covered by a retirement plan, your IRA is tax deductible, regardless of your combined income.

2. If you are working and your company offers a retirement plan such as a 401(k) that you have not joined because your husband has a plan, reconsider. If you are self-employed, start a Keogh plan. You and your husband may decide that you have $3,000 a year to invest in your combined plans. Do not have all of the money go into your husband's account. You are working and you should have your own account.

3. If you have a pension plan at your company and you leave to have a baby or to change jobs, you may be given a payout of your pension money. Frequently women do not invest that money in a roll-over IRA because it seems like an insignificant amount. If you don't roll over your distribution into an IRA, you have to pay taxes on it as income. Remember, left to accumulate that money can mount up. If you receive a pension payout as a distribution, immediately put it into a roll-over IRA.

4. If your husband already has a pension plan, there is nothing wrong with you having one too. That way, you are each protected.

If your husband works for a large company he will probably have some combination of benefits of this type.

SMART CHOICES

While the money in many benefit plans is invested by your employer, the trend lately has been a shift to defined contribution plans, which shift the decision-making responsibility to the employee. With defined benefit plans, your employer has to guarantee a certain result. With a defined contribution, the result could depend on your investment know-how.

Your employer may have opened the 401(k) through a mutual fund organization; your IRA may be with your local bank. No matter; you will need some basic investment strategy.

TAKING IT OUT WHEN RETIREMENT FINALLY COMES: IT'S NOT TAX FREE

When you and your husband retire, you may receive your retirement money as either a fixed monthly benefit—the usual way for pensions that are defined benefit—or as a lump-sum distribution from your company's retirement plan. If you receive a lump sum, you have just sixty days to make a critical decision. You and your husband can pay taxes on the money or you can defer taxes by putting the money into a special IRA called a rollover IRA. To decide requires careful analysis of the tax benefits of either choice. If either your company or your husband's gives a seminar on retirement tax planning, you should attend. If not, you should probably consult a professional. A mistake can be very costly.

Be sure to find out about Social Security integration. Social Security integration means that your employer can reduce what the company pays you by the amount you will get from Social Security; up to 50 percent of your pension can be deducted this way. If you and your husband are counting on both Social Security and pension income, be sure you check on this.

DON'T WAIVE GOOD-BYE TO YOUR PENSION

Since 1974 a series of laws has gradually mandated a spouse's right to share in a pension fund. If your husband has a private pension plan that is paid out in the form of a fixed monthly benefit you are also entitled to some benefits. When Congress passed the Employee Retirement Income Security Act (ERISA) in 1974 pension plans were required to provide married workers with survivors' benefits that must equal no less than half the retired worker's benefits. The trouble with the original law was that a husband did not have to tell his wife what he had done. Many widows discovered that their husband's pensions stopped when their husbands died. Since 1984 you and your husband must make this decision together. The law calls for a pension to be paid out as either a joint and survivor benefit or as a single benefit. If the benefit is a "single" benefit, it is higher than if it is a joint and survivor benefit. The single benefit stops with the death of the worker. The joint and survivor benefit pays a lower rate but continues during the lifetime of the nonworking spouse as well. Your husband cannot make the decision himself to choose a single benefit, leaving you without any benefits.

There are several ways you can receive your joint and survivor benefits. Here's a typical example. If the maximum payment for a pension is $3,500 per month, then a 50 percent survivor's payment might give a couple $3,000 a month, and when the husband died the wife would receive $1,500 monthly.

Some financial planners suggest that couples, when deciding whether to have a single, larger benefit or a joint and survivor benefit, which means a lower payout, also consider a plan known as pension maximization. It sounds great. You and your husband agree that you will take the higher monthly payout of your husband's pension. Then from the higher proceeds you buy a life insurance policy that will pay off when your husband dies.

There are several potential problems with this. The first problem is that you and your husband just might not get around to buying the insurance policy. There is also a chance that the price of the insurance will go up and you will not be able to get the amount you thought you could get.

Pension "max," as it is known, makes sense if you, the wife, have a pension plan that pays more than your husband's. You take the larger payout. Then buy an insurance policy on your life, which is a much cheaper policy because you are probably younger. Be very careful about signing off on a joint and survivor annuity under your husband's plan. The above is a simplified explanation of how pension plans and Social Security pay benefits. Every plan is different in its details.

While the federal pension laws protect the wife or

husband whose benefits are paid out in fixed monthly series, some lump-sum distributions are not subject to such scrutiny. Your husband can take his money and run. If he is smart, however, he will put his lump-sum distribution into a rollover IRA while the two of you decide which is the best option for your money.

You can invest it in mutual funds, you can buy an annuity from an insurance company that will guarantee a fixed sum over a fixed period of years, or you can do a little of each. The main point is that you want the money to be around for both of you, and this requires careful planning.

THE HIGH COST OF MOTHERHOOD

When it comes to pensions, despite all the books that speak about you and your spouse, for women, the future can seem bleak. The higher wages and longer years of work that men experience and the lower wages and interrupted work years of most women culminate not surprisingly in gaps in their pension income when they retire. Consider the statistics: just 22 percent of women over sixty-five receive private pension benefits. The average private pension account for women was $3,651 in 1991. For men the figure is substantially higher, $7,059.[7]

More women are employed in jobs that are not covered by pension plans. Women average 11.5 years away from the labor force; men average 1.3 years away.[8] A typical example is the woman who has worked for a few years. She leaves her job to have a baby. If she has begun putting money into a pension plan, chances are she has not worked long enough to assure a permanent pension (known as "vesting," regardless of whether you return to work for the same employer). If you leave a job and are not vested, you frequently get back your accrued benefits in a lump sum. If you act quickly (within sixty days) and put the money into an IRA, you pay no taxes and can continue to build a retirement war chest. If you spend the money instead to buy a new car, you have to pay taxes on the money and also a penalty for taking your money out of the pension plan early. Only 13 percent of the people under fifty-five who get lump-sum distributions put their money into IRAs. Since women are more frequent job changers they are more likely to lose out on building pensions.

Many women work part-time, not enough hours to be included in the pension plans of their companies. You must work at least twenty hours a week to be eligible for most company pension plans. Many women work in service industries that are least likely to have pension funds. There are no pension funds for the housewife.

If you have moved into formerly male-dominated work areas you are more likely to be covered. There tends to be greater pension coverage in older industries—manufacturing, mining, and communications. Retail business and other service businesses, such as finance and real estate, often do not provide pensions.[9]

Many women take off critical early years of their working lives in order to raise their children. But it is in those early years that they could be investing, letting their money accumulate. If you enter the workplace later in life, you've missed those capital building years.

Here's what I mean. If your husband started work when he was twenty-one and contributed $2,000 a year to a retirement savings plan for ten years tax deferred, he would have put into his account a grand total of $20,000. But if that money accumulated at 10 percent a year, when he was sixty-five he would have $985,387. You, on the other hand, take those first ten years of your life together to raise a few children. You don't start working until you are thirty-one. You put $2,000 a year into your account every year until you reach age sixty-five. At the end of that time, you would have put in actual dollars $68,000 into your account. If your money accumulated tax deferred at the same 10 percent, you would have $596,254. (For a look at how this really works, see the table on page 135.)

Clearly, the husband who starts early and lets his money accumulate in a retirement plan has a great advantage over the wife who delays her career. And this doesn't even consider the years you have lost in building your career. There's nothing wrong with making this kind of choice. What's wrong is then thinking you should not have a say in the spending of the money that your husband has been making.

To a great degree, pensions in most families are in the husband's name. The wife is either not working or works in a business that doesn't have a pension. Husbands have control of retirement planning. Frequently, pension planning for the wife is nonexistent; she gets survivor's benefits. As more women work and move into management positions in their companies, much of this disparity should change.

If you and your husband both work and have pensions,

The High Cost of Motherhood:
At a 10 Percent Yield, Who Has More at 65?*

| | HUSBAND | | WIFE | |
AGE	CONTRIBU- TIONS	VALUE AT YR. END	CONTRIBU- TIONS	VALUE AT YR. END
21	$2,000	$2,200		$0
22	$2,000	$4,620		$0
23	$2,000	$7,282		$0
24	$2,000	$10,210		$0
25	$2,000	$13,431		$0
26	$2,000	$16,974		$0
27	$2,000	$20,872		$0
28	$2,000	$25,159		$0
29	$2,000	$29,875		$0
30	$2,000	$35,062		$0
31		$38,569	$2,000	$2,200
32		$42,425	$2,000	$4,620
33		$46,668	$2,000	$7,282
34		$51,335	$2,000	$10,210
35		$56,468	$2,000	$13,431
36		$62,115	$2,000	$16,974
37		$68,327	$2,000	$20,872
38		$75,159	$2,000	$25,159
39		$82,675	$2,000	$29,875
40		$90,943	$2,000	$35,062
41		$100,037	$2,000	$40,769
42		$110,041	$2,000	$47,045
43		$121,045	$2,000	$53,950
44		$133,149	$2,000	$61,545
45		$146,464	$2,000	$69,899
46		$161,110	$2,000	$79,089
47		$177,222	$2,000	$89,198
48		$194,944	$2,000	$100,318
49		$214,438	$2,000	$112,550
50		$235,882	$2,000	$126,005
51		$259,470	$2,000	$140,805
52		$285,417	$2,000	$157,086
53		$313,959	$2,000	$174,995
54		$345,355	$2,000	$194,694
55		$379,890	$2,000	$216,364
56		$417,879	$2,000	$240,200
57		$459,667	$2,000	$266,420
58		$505,634	$2,000	$295,262
59		$556,197	$2,000	$326,988
60		$611,817	$2,000	$361,887
61		$672,998	$2,000	$400,276
62		$740,298	$2,000	$442,503
63		$814,328	$2,000	$488,953
64		$895,761	$2,000	$540,049
65		$985,337	$2,000	$596,254
TOTAL	$20,000	$985,337	$70,000	$596,254

*Figures provided by Gary J Strum, senior vice president, Quest for Value
Distribution.

you have an opportunity to build your retirement plans together.

MARRIED: HOW TO BLEND YOUR BENEFITS

1. Each of you should get copies of your benefit plan, IRA statements, and Social Security benefits.
2. If you both have pension plans be sure to check the beneficiaries. Naming a spouse is mandatory under some plans, unless you both sign waivers. You might want to leave your pension to your mother, but your husband would have to agree. For some plans you need a waiver, but on others—for example, IRAs—this is not mandatory. One woman's husband died and when she inquired about collecting his benefits, discovered that another woman already had. If you were previously married and your former husband is named as the beneficiary for a qualified pension plan, even though your current husband is entitled to collect survivor benefits, not changing the name could result in frustrating delays.
3. Find out what kinds of plans you both have available from your companies; if neither one of you has started to take advantage of retirement planning, get started. Consider building your retirement plans fifty-fifty. Otherwise you could end up with lopsided estates and have tax-planning problems

   Some companies make matching grants. If your husband's company matches contributions and gives fifty cents for every dollar he contributes and your company is only giving twenty-five cents on every dollar, it may seem wiser to put money into your husband's plan. But you should participate in your own company plan as well.

If you think you will take time off from your job to have children, start investing in your pension plan as soon as possible. Your money will accumulate tax deferred while you are not working.

If your company does not have a pension plan, contribute to an IRA, even if you have to do it with after-tax dollars.

4. If you and your husband have a long-term plan to buy a house, you can borrow against some pension plans. Check the loan provisions of the plans you are offered. If one of you has a loan provision in your plan, you might want to put more of your assets into the company plan with the loan provision. (Also note that your husband can borrow against a 401(k) plan without telling you. Naturally, you can do the same.)

5. Have a joint investment strategy. If your husband can only invest in fixed income through his plan, perhaps your plan can be put into equities to give you more investment flexibility. You and your husband should check the mix on a regular basis.

6. Know the payout choices. If you and your husband have defined benefit plans they must offer joint and survivor options. This means that when you are ready to retire you will have the choice of having your full benefits paid to each of you, or else you will each get reduced benefits paid in your lifetime and benefits that will continue to be paid to your spouse when you die. If your husband's full benefit is $20,000 he would get

that until he died, then his pension would stop completely. You would have just your own full benefit until you died. If you took a full benefit and your husband took a reduced benefit, you would continue to receive part of his benefits once you were on your own. Of course we never know who will die first, so a third option is for each of you to take a reduced payout.

7. You should also check out the payout options for any tax planning you might want to do. The type of distribution can make a difference in your tax planning. Remember, a big chunk of retirement income is taxable—all that tax-deferred money that you've been accumulating.

8. Be sure to find out whether your benefits or his are integrated with Social Security. If they are, your benefits will be reduced by the amount you receive from Social Security, *up to 50 percent of your total benefit.*

9. Check out the life insurance provisions of your pension plans. You might be able to buy life insurance at a good rate from your company. Also check whether the insurance would be transferrable if you leave your job. You might want to have some life insurance of your own. If you have a defined benefit plan and your husband dies before he reaches the age of fifty-five, his earliest retirement age, you might not get much of a payout. Life insurance, at least term, is a must in these cases. Term insurance is insurance purchased on a year-by-year basis. It does not accumulate any benefits and must be repurchased each year. The younger you are, the lower the premium. Term insurance, when you are young, is much less expensive than whole life.

10. Second marriages are a bit tricky. You and your husband may each have pensions that you would like to leave to your children from a first marriage. You might each want to waive your survivor rights as beneficiaries of each other's plans. Some couples even include such waivers in prenuptial agreements.

If this is a second marriage for your husband, find out if he has already promised part of his pension benefits to his first wife.

SAVINGS AND INVESTMENTS: THE THIRD PART OF YOUR RETIREMENT PLAN

If you and your husband have anything at all left over after putting money into your IRAs, Keoghs, 401(k) plans, and other tax-deferred investments, you will probably want to do some additional investing. Actually, your savings and investments should be a part of your retirement planning, because you probably will not have enough money if you rely on Social Security and your pension plans.

Women tend to let their husbands take over. Maybe it's tradition, because there is no evidence that women do not become successful money managers. In fact, where is the evidence that men are better? One woman was married to a CPA. She just assumed he knew what he was doing. When, sadly, he had a stroke, she was forced to take over the family finances. To her surprise, and that of her college-age son, she did much better than her husband. But don't wait for your husband to have a stroke. If you really know nothing about investing, take a course or begin reading some magazines. *Money* is a good one. Begin reading the business and finance pages of your newspapers. And use your own common sense. If you plan to hire a broker, both you and your husband should be in on the interview. Ask friends for recommendations—friends who are in similar financial situations. If you don't have millions, don't choose a broker who only handles accounts for the very rich.

If you are really a neophyte, think about beginning to invest through mutual funds. But be sure you participate. Don't be intimidated. Ask even dumb questions. And if you don't like the answers don't invest. If someone promises too much too fast, zip your wallet and run. Don't invest because you heard that someone else did. Do your own homework. Understand what you are doing.

A SHORT GUIDE TO INVESTMENTS

First of all, you have to define the purpose of your investments. Of course, the primary purpose is to have more money, but sometimes you may be able to further refine your goals:

1. money for your old age
2. capital for a major project—a house, a business
3. money to leave for your children

The best way to achieve your goal has historically been investing in common stocks. Most people believe common stocks are risky because the value of stocks can fall. A stock is really a share in the ownership of a company. Stocks usually go up if a company does well, and down if a company does badly. Many people believe that by buying bonds that will pay a set rate of interest they are not taking any risk. A bond is really a loan that you are making to someone, either a corporation or a government agency or even Uncle Sam. You lend your money; in return you get back a set amount of interest over a fixed number of years. It is true that if you buy a bond for $1,000 (the usual price for a bond) and hold it for ten years, you will at the end of those ten years get back your $1,000, but depending upon the rate of inflation, your money will have lost some of its purchasing power.

To preserve buying power you must receive a return that is more than the inflation rate. If inflation is 5 percent, you must earn more than 5 percent. Anything over 5 percent is your real profit. When we have low inflation and high bond yields, as we did in the late 1980s, bonds were a safe and profitable investment. When we had high inflation and low bond yields, as we did in the 1970s, bonds were a bad investment. In the 1990s bond yields have been low but so has inflation. Bonds have been a less than ideal investment and many investors have turned to equities in the hopes of a higher return.

When you are young and are still earning money, you can afford to take more risk with your money. The older you are, however, the less concerned you may be with preserving the purchasing power of your money over a long-term period. Then bonds can also be a way to invest, because you know you will have a fixed rate of return that you can depend on every month. If you are not worried about leaving a lot of your money to your children you can also spend some of your money and not worry that at the end of ten years you will have less.

If you have an investment adviser with whom you feel comfortable and with whom you have worked in the past, there is no reason not to continue. If you and your husband have a broker, you should get to know the broker or adviser; don't wait for something to go wrong.

If you have never invested, do not know an adviser, and suddenly receive a lump sum (life insurance checks could come within a month after your husband's death), put your money into a money market fund. Make sure it is one run by a large company, such as Fidelity or Dreyfus. You will receive interest and can take time deciding how you want to invest the money.

If the lump sum is a part of a pension split in a divorce, you can put that money into an IRA and keep the money tax deferred.

If you are ready to think about investing, try to define your goals. Then think about how you will invest. To me, mutual funds are the easiest and least expensive way to do this. There are two types of mutual funds: no-load funds, for which you do not pay a purchase fee, and load funds, which charge a commission. Load funds are usually sold by a broker, while no load funds are sold directly by the company that manages the fund. Many funds now charge 12b-1 fees, which add a yearly fee to the cost of a fund. Check the fee structure before making a decision. Then you must evaluate the performance of the fund, minus the cost of the fees you will have to pay. Many people say only choose no-load, but I think the most important feature in choosing a fund is how well the fund performs.

Money magazine and *Forbes* rate various mutual funds every year. This will give you an idea of past performance of the funds, but, needless to say, is not an indication of how well the funds will do in the future.

Once you have the information, purchase a small amount of one of the funds that seems to best fit your goals. Do not invest more than 20 percent of your capital. Choose a big mutual fund company with a track record, even though no past record can tell you what will happen in the future.

The best type of common stock funds are those that provide some growth and income.

After you have put your first 20 percent to work, you can divide another 40 percent between two more funds so that you will have a total of 60 percent of your money invested in stocks. If this makes you nervous put only 50 or 55 percent of your money in common stocks.

Place 30 or 40 percent of your money in bond funds. There are many types of bond funds. You can buy government bond funds, municipal bond funds (usually tax free, and so pay a lower rate of interest) high-yield bond funds, and junk bond funds. The main point is to split your money in a few funds and to buy from big, well-known companies.

The remaining 10 percent of your money can be kept in a money market fund so you have immediate money should you need it.

You will be unlikely to get rich on this type of investing, but you will be able to sleep well at night and over the years will probably make a small profit above the rate of inflation.

This is a simple scheme. Your brother-in-law in the investment business will probably tell you to give him the money to invest for you. Don't do it.

One secret of successful investing is letting your money grow over a long period. It's not the only way to invest, but I think it is the best way for people who know little about the market.

HOW A FINANCIAL PLANNER CAN HELP

One way to plan for retirement is to visit a financial planner. The cost can range from a few hundred to a few thousand dollars, depending on the complexity of your assets. You can do it yourself with a workbook or plan provided by firms such as T. Rowe Price or Fidelity. WealthBuilder is a popular computer program that you can use. If you don't know too much about your retirement plans and your husband doesn't like to talk about it—because he doesn't like to think about retiring—suggesting that you visit a planner might be a great idea. Often a concerned wife brings her husband to a planner. Many planners will not see a husband without his wife or a wife without her husband. Word of mouth and company recommendations are good ways to find a planner. Remember, however, that this is an unlicensed field; just about anyone can hang up a financial-planning sign. Financial planners generally work in two different ways. One group charges a fee and does not sell products. The other group is usually affiliated with a company—either insurance or brokerage or tax shelter—and offers free advice, hoping to recoup on the products you subsequently buy. My own bias would be for the fee without the products.

Financial planning really forces you to focus on facts. The planning process can also bring out some hidden conflicts. Some of the problems are the recurrent financial fights in a marriage: you want to spend money on curtains, your husband wants to spend money on a wine refrigerator. But often deeper conflicts are revealed. One planner told of a husband who didn't want to have life insurance for his wife because he didn't "want some other guy spending his money." Sometimes, when a wife begins her career later in life than her husband, especially if she is a few years younger than he, she may not want to retire at all, preferring to continue working.

How much money you actually have, how much money you will need for retirement, and how you will get there are the basic questions of the planning business. The planner will need to know your expected Social Security and pension benefits as well as your other savings and investments. Computers make it easy to project a series of numbers to find out that you will need a certain amount of income when you retire. When you work with a planner you have to understand the assumptions.

While there are more scientific ways to figure out how much income you will need in order to retire, here are some guidelines. You will probably need 70 percent of the average of the last three years of your preretirement income. Of this, 15 percent will come from Social Security, and between 30 and 35 percent from a pension plan. The remaining dollars will have to come from investments. Planners use a rate of inflation and a rate of interest to figure out how much money you will need when you retire. They also use actuarial tables to figure out how many years you can expect to live.

You should know what those assumptions are in order to evaluate any advice you get.

QUESTIONS TO ASK A FINANCIAL PLANNER

1. What is the assumed rate of inflation?
2. What is the assumed rate of growth in assets?
3. What is the assumed yield?
4. Does the plan include spending assets?
5. Is the income taxable?

These questions are important. In this age of computers, numbers can do almost anything. Here's an example:

You and your husband would like to retire in eleven years with an annual income of $50,000 (70 percent of your current $70,000 income). The financial planner does a bit of calculating and determines that you would need $89,793 if we have an inflation rate of 5 percent. Lately inflation has been low, but think back and remember what inflation was like a few years ago. Then ask the planner to tell you what would happen if inflation was higher or lower. Here is a little chart that will illustrate what the change in numbers can mean for that $50,000:

Your retirement income in 2005 dollars:	3% inflation	5% inflation	9% inflation
	$71,288	$89,793	$140,633

The planner looks at the amount of money you and your husband have socked away in savings and pensions and tells you that in order to get that $89,793 in eleven years, you would need a nest egg of $1.8 million if you could be assured of a 5 percent yield. But if you knew you could get 10 percent you would only need $1.1 million. The amount you have already saved will then be subtracted from the amount you will need. The planner will then suggest several ways to close the gap. You can decide you will manage on less. You can increase the amount of money you are putting away.

Many people consider buying annuities for their retirement. These are purchased from insurance companies. They function a little like pension plans in that you can build up tax-deferred investments that can begin paying money to you when you are ready to retire. You can buy fixed annuities, which pay a fixed rate; or you can buy variable rate annuities, which pay depending on how well the investments have performed.

There are a few drawbacks to buying annuities. They are expensive because there are high sales commissions and maintenance charges. Your money is locked away. And you have to be careful that the company offering them will be solvent when you are ready to retire.

Why bother to have them? They do offer the tax-deferred advantages of pension plans. They are a way to supplement a retirement account.

Other choices include deciding that you will sell your house and invest that money, assuming you can rent for less money than you could make by investing the proceeds from the sale of your house. You can also get a reverse mortgage that allows you to take money out based on the value of your house. You can decide that you will spend assets. This is known as spending down. You start with a fixed sum and then withdraw a certain amount each year, until you are left with zero. For example, if you started with $50,000 and withdrew $580 each month, your money would last for 10 years.[10]

There are several problems with financial planning.

Most financial plans do not take into account the likelihood of inflation eroding your standard of living because the plan never projects an increase in income while you are retired. If inflation is 7 percent, purchasing power will erode by half in just ten years. Nor does the plan usually project, as has happened in the early 1990s, a precipitous drop in interest rates. When this happens, projected income fails to materialize. Social Security does give you a cost-of-living increase, but the rule that most planners follow is that Social Security will only provide about 10 to 15 percent of your retirement income.

The second problem is that the plan changes when one of you dies. The early retirement years will probably be shared. Your Social Security and his, your pension plan and his, your joint investments—if you and your husband both worked and retire, you will each receive your maximum pension benefits; you will each get Social Security. If your husband dies, you will get your own Social Security. His will be discontinued. Your pension plan income will continue, and you will get the "survivor" benefits from his pension plan. If you never worked and your husband retires, you will still receive benefits from his Social Security and his pension plan. If your husband dies, however, you will receive smaller benefits from each, because you have no benefits of your own.

You, the wife, have to know what will happen to your income when you are alone. The purchasing power of the income you receive, unless your benefits are indexed to inflation as they are in Social Security, will erode. For women in second marriages, there are even greater problems because frequently some portion of their husbands' estates will be headed for his children from his first marriage. One financial planner who frequently works with couples getting ready to retire reports that discussing this with couples can lead to tremendous arguments.

UNINTENDED RETIREMENT

The 1990s began with a recession that ended in 1992, but the fallout to business continued. It is not unusual to pick up the paper and read a headline that says Corporation X will lay off 3,000 people. Yet few people are prepared for the financial dislocation this can cause. Of course, there is severance pay, usually tied to the length of time you have worked for the company. And, depending on the size of the company, there may be such "perks" as outplacement services and even the use of an office for a period of time.

If you and your husband work, it is your husband who is likely to lose his job. What would happen to your finances if either of you were out of work for an extended period of time? Expenses don't change that much. Know how many weeks of severance pay you get. Know the expenses of finding another job. What happens to your health insurance?

You need savings and investments to see you through a crisis. Above all, you have to be supportive of each other. The wife who doesn't understand the finances can be a burden in troubled times. The wife who knows can help her husband.

Disability is another possible problem many couples may face. Sometimes, whatever you do, the unforeseen will arise. While it is hard to be prepared for all of life's blows, there are a few that can be softened.

When my friend Mary Green's husband was sixty, he

suffered a stroke. She was suddenly plunged into a world of hospitals, doctors, and therapists. Fortunately, they had medical insurance. But as time elapsed and the expenses continued to mount, the medical insurance covered less and less. The insurance company rules changed. The insurance company did not pay for private care. She had to hire nurses round-the-clock. She spent a lot of money on therapy, but her husband never regained his faculties.

Because her husband had the stroke before his sixty-fifth birthday, he was forced to retire with less than maximum pension benefits. Money became a problem. The income from her husband's two pension plans was not sufficient to cover expenses.

After some research, Mary Green found a solution. She sold their house and moved to a life care facility; another name is continuing care retirement community (CCRC). This is not a cheap or risk-free solution to your problems. You pay a lot to enter and then pay high monthly fees for services that can include meals, nursing care, and hospital availability. In 1988 the average entry fee was $45,000, and the monthly fee average was $715. (A booklet that could be helpful is *Selecting Retirement Housing,* available free from AARP Fulfillment, 601 E Street N.W., Washington, D.C. 20049.) Basically, life care facilities are a combination of retirement village and convalescent home. The big advantage of a life care facility is that once you have paid your dues, you can't be turned out.

Of course, not all disability is permanent. Divorce lawyer Raoul Felder may be accused of carving up his opponents in a courtroom, but when it came to carving a chicken he wasn't as skilled. While attempting to dismember the bird, he dropped a carving knife on his foot. The resulting injury kept him out of the courtroom for four months. With disability insurance, Felder was able to replace some of his lost income.

While the term "disability" has a variety of synonyms—including disadvantage, drawback, and handicap—the word has taken on a specific meaning in the lexicon of the American working world. It means to be hurt—either from illness or accident—in some way that means you can no longer work.

What are the odds that this will happen to your husband?

If your husband is over twenty-one, there's a one-in-three chance that he will become disabled at some time.

If your husband is forty or under, he is three times more likely to have a disability than he is to die.

If your husband is between the ages of thirty-five and sixty-five the chances of being unable to work for ninety days or more because of a disabling illness or injury are about equal to your chances of dying. "A twenty-five-year-old professional male stands a 34.8 percent chance of suffering a long-term disability by age sixty-five, and the average duration of the disability is twenty-six months. The odds decrease each year, reaching 17.6 percent by age fifty-five, but the average duration increases to fifty-three months."[11]

WHAT YOU SHOULD KNOW IF YOUR HUSBAND CAN'T WORK

Does he have disability insurance? This insurance pays you some portion of your "earned income" should you be unable to work for a period of time. Disability insurance is income replacement. The standard rule is insurance covers 60 percent of what would have been your monthly income. If your husband pays the premium, the income is not taxable. If his employer pays the premium, the income is taxable. Fewer than 20 percent of companies with 100 or fewer employees offer disability insurance.[12]

Find out the terms of your husband's disability insurance. How long must your husband be out of work before he will collect any money at all? Usually the longer you must be out of work before payments start, the lower the premium. Standard waiting times are between one month—the highest premium—and three months.

What percentage of his salary will be replaced by the disability payments? One couple was devastated to discover that the husband's disability insurance covered only his regular salary and not the bonus that he thought was part of his yearly earnings.

If your husband doesn't have disability insurance you may belong to a group that makes it available to its members. For example, the Archaeological Institute of America recently offered its members a disability insurance policy with a yearly premium of $47.50 for $500 in monthly benefits for those under thirty. As with most disability insurance there were restrictions and waiting periods.

Will your husband be eligible for Social Security payments as a result of his disability? You have to be unable to work for at least a year to qualify. Only about 20 percent of all disability claims are approved by Social Security.

What other sources of income do you have? Does your husband have a pension plan? If so, find out when he will be eligible to collect this and what percentage of his salary he will receive. Can he borrow against it?

Do you have a durable power of attorney that will allow you to act for your husband? If you don't and your property in not in joint name, you could spend time getting the court to appoint you as guardian. This could be granted as emergency powers, but it's much better to have a power of attorney on hand. You can prepare a power of attorney yourself by buying a form from a stationery store and then having it notarized. You should also have a durable power of attorney allowing your husband to act for you. (By the way, if you are taking care of elderly parents, be sure you have their signed durable powers of attorney.)

If your husband stops working because of a disability will you still be able to get medical insurance?

If your husband must stop working and he owns the company, how will the other employees be paid? If your husband has a small business, business overhead insurance, often referred to as key man insurance, covers rents, utilities, and salaries.

Of course, women can have accidents or get sick as well. And women are far less likely to have employee paid disability insurance. If you are working, you should also have some disability insurance to replace your lost income should something happen to you.

MEDICAL INSURANCE

Medical expenses are the wild card of retirement and old age.

Medicare is the federal government's health insurance program that provides medical insurance to those over sixty-five who are eligible for Social Security. Medicare is divided into two parts: Part A pays hospital insurance; part B pays doctor's bills. There is a monthly premium for part B. However, Medicare does not make any provisions for two of the largest expenses of old age—prescription medicines and custodial nursing home care. Medicare does cover nursing home care if it is rehabilitative. If you are hospitalized because you broke your hip and then must go to a nursing home, your bills would be paid by Medicare. Medicare does not pay for general dental work or foot care, both frequent problems as we age.

Many people choose to buy Medigap insurance. Medigap is private insurance available to pay for costs not covered by Medicare such as prescription medicine, hospital deductibles, a private-duty nurse in the hospital, and personal care at home. Ten different standardized Medigap plans are available through private insurers.

Then there's Medicaid, a program meant for the needy which does provide nursing home coverage, but does not provide total health care. In order to qualify for Medicaid, however, you must have very few assets. Although Medicaid is a federal program it is administered by each state. State laws of eligibility vary. In some states the aid is provided only to those sixty-five or over or to disabled persons of any age. Other states allow Medicaid to be given in special situations where there are very high medical expenses to those whose income might otherwise disqualify them. The restrictions have led many people to protest that our national health care should provide more coverage. So far this is not a reality.

The best protection is to do it yourself. For most women, the preparation should mean a realistic look once again at the family assets. But this time you have to look at the possibility that an illness of your husband's will use up much of your combined assets, leaving you unable to get the care you need if you become ill. If you haven't gotten it by now, let me tell you once again: Women tend to outlive men. Women remain widows an average of fifteen years. By the year 2000, estimates project there will be 7.4 million widows; you may be among them. So you should be sure to check on nursing home insurance (see below) and life insurance for your husband.

Nursing Homes: The Facts

By the third millennium over eight million Americans over the age of sixty-five will probably need some form of long-term care because of chronic illness. Of this group, 70 percent will probably be cared for by a family member—most probably you, the wife.

In 1990, 1.5 million people over sixty-five were in nursing homes. Seventy-five percent of them were women. Two out of five people aged sixty-five or more risk entering a nursing home. The average length of stay in a nursing home is 2.5 years. Approximately 5 percent of the over-sixty-five population are now in nursing homes. About 25 percent of those over eighty-five live in nursing homes.

Nursing homes are not inexpensive. Costs vary from state to state. An average yearly cost could be $40,000. If you want deluxe care the price soars.

As more Americans live longer there has been a change in attitude about who should have to care for so many old folks. In the past it was considered normal for families to take care of their own. Now that isn't possible for many, leaving nursing home care the only option. The high cost of medical care means that funds are often spent for the husband's care, leaving the wife with a reduced income while her husband is ill, and even fewer assets to help her out when she is alone.

For a large part of the middle class, the money spent is part of the family's life savings. It may be a great part of what a couple had planned to bequeath to their children.

Many Americans think the government should pay for long-term care. Elder-care lawyers have developed strategies for clients to give away assets in order to qualify for Medicaid, which does pay for nursing home care. But in 1993 Congress passed laws that enable states to attempt to recover money that was transferred to take advantage of Medicaid. For more information write to The National Academy of Elder Law Attorneys, Inc., 655 N. Alvernon Way, Suite 108, Tuscon, Arizona 85711.

SHOULD YOU PROTECT YOUR ASSETS AND QUALIFY
FOR MEDICAID-FUNDED NURSING HOME CARE?

Several different strategies have evolved to help couples
who would like to be able to qualify for publicly funded
Medicaid to pay for nursing home care. Most of the
Medicaid planning strategies involve giving up assets
before you need nursing home care. Usually this involves
creating trusts which transfer assets from one spouse to
the other or from a couple to their children. Each state
has a different standard.

Other solutions to the Medicaid qualifying problem
include putting assets into annuities payable to the wife,
whose income is not counted toward Medicaid eligibility,
or putting assets into the family home, which does not
count as an asset when computing your net worth for
Medicaid. Oh yes, if you own your own burial plot that
is not counted toward Medicaid eligibility.

Another possibility is to transfer all the assets to the
healthy spouse, usually the wife, who then refuses to pay
for her husband's nursing home care.

Some couples have taken an even more drastic step.
Transferring all assets to the wife, for example, then getting a divorce. The sick husband can therefore be whisked
straight to a nursing home paid for by Medicaid.

Of course, it isn't always the husband who gets sick. It
can be the wife. This creates other problems, especially
if the husband is older and realizes that he will not be
around to take care of his wife and wants to be sure she
will receive proper care should he die first.

Here is one way to handle that problem. Some couples

have created so-called irrevocable Medicaid trusts that place assets out of reach but allow income and dividends to be received, thus allowing either husband or wife to qualify for Medicaid. The remainder of the trust usually would go to the couple's children. As of August 10, 1993, the law changed slightly, making the validity of trusts created after that date ambiguous.

Solutions to long-term care involving Medicaid are uncertain and involve giving up control of assets, something that may be psychologically and practically undesirable. What happens, for example, if your children divorce, are sued, or just spend your money? After all, you saved your money to take care of yourself in case of a rainy day, and, in a way, having to be in a nursing home is a rainy day. It's what you hoped would never happen, but if it does, maybe the money should be spent to assure your care. This is a question every couple will have to discuss and decide together with a qualified lawyer.

NURSING HOME INSURANCE

Of course, you can also prepare for the unwelcome by buying nursing home insurance. Nursing home insurance is a recent addition to the panoply of products peddled by insurance salespeople. If carefully chosen, it allows you the luxury of not worrying about being able to afford a nursing home.

Those who might benefit from nursing home insurance would be families with a net worth of between $250,000 and $400,000. If you get it before age sixty-five your premium will be much lower; it goes up as you get older. The biggest purchasers are usually those between sixty-five and seventy-nine. You can't buy it when you are over eighty.

The average premium is between $1200 and $4000 per year, which will probably pay as much as 80 percent of the cost. There are some pitfalls when buying nursing home insurance.[13] Insurance companies can claim all information was not supplied. Worse, the insurance company can go bankrupt.

Here's what to look for in nursing home insurance: First make sure the company is rated by A. M. Best, the leading insurance rating company, with a rating of A+ or A. Next see that the daily benefit is at least $100 with inflation protection and a minimum benefit period of two years. Normally, there will be a waiting period of ninety to one hundred days before your benefits begin. The longer the period that you wait before collecting, the lower your premium. Be sure that there is no prior hospitalization requirement—i.e., you don't have to first be in a hospital before going to the nursing home. And, finally, there should be no requirement of prior skilled care.[14]

Ten Things Every Woman Should Know When Her Husband Retires

1. Should your husband continue to pay for life insurance? Of course a lot depends on your current assets.
2. Decide whether you will need nursing home insurance—usually recommended in cases of a net worth between $250,000 and $400,000. Remember the younger you are when you buy it, the cheaper your premiums.
3. If your husband would like to take a single annuity

payout, instead of a joint but lower payout, be sure that you will be able to continue medical insurance and that you will have enough income.

4. If your husband chooses a single life annuity remember that when you are alone you will receive no money from his pension.

5. Be careful of something called pension max (choosing a single annuity payment which gives you more money with the idea that you can then buy life insurance and still have more money to spend than if you chose a joint payout).

6. If you are working and not yet ready to retire, be very careful of retiring before you are eligible for maximum pension benefits.

7. Remember that all the money you and your husband spend together during retirement means there will be less for you when you are, as is more than likely, alone.

8. Remember that inflation, even at 5 percent, means the cost of everything will double in fourteen years.

9. If your husband is anxious to give everything to your children or, if it's a second marriage, his children, be careful. They may not help you when you need it.

10. Don't underestimate the amount of money you will both need when you retire.

Many women still think they do not have to plan for their own retirement—that their husbands will provide. When it comes to pensions, savings, and other plans for the future, every woman should know what her husband has and should plan for her own future as well.

8.
Will Power: The American Way of Leaving

What do John Lennon and Jacqueline Kennedy Onassis have in common? For one thing, they were both very rich when they died. Even more important, they both wrote wills.

Mrs. Onassis's was an elaborate document, with trusts and specific personal bequests. For instance, she left a copy of her husband John F. Kennedy's inaugural address, signed by Robert Frost, to Alexander Forger, her lawyer. She left her Fifth Avenue apartment to her children, Caroline Kennedy Schlossberg and John Kennedy, Jr. And to Maurice Tempelsman, the man who had been her companion for fifteen years, she left an ancient Greek head of a woman. She also established a charitable foundation and named her children as two of the trustees, bidding them give contributions to charities that would make a difference in the "cultural or social betterment of mankind or the relief of human suffering." In short, this was the will of a wealthy woman who had given a great deal of thought to how she wanted to distribute the estimated $200 million she was leaving behind.

John Lennon, as we all know, died in his prime. His will was simple. He left almost everything to his wife, Yoko Ono. His will was the will of a man who had probably not spent a great deal of time thinking about the dispersal of his property. John Lennon was not atypical.

The oldest known will is that of Uah, an Egyptian who lived in the third millennium, B.C. American wills are rooted in the Anglo-Saxon tradition, as are much of our marital traditions. One of the earliest English wills on record was written by a wealthy woman named Wolgith way back in the eleventh century. Evidently a woman of considerable property, she divvied up her vast estates between her numerous children and her church—and offered up a solemn curse to any who would try and contest her wishes.

A will is the official document that tells the government and the public what to do with your property when you die. If you die without a will—*intestate* is the legal term—your property will be distributed in accordance with the laws of the state where you live. Federal laws do not govern wills, although the federal government swoops in to collect taxes on large estates.

Some couples think that if you do not have a will, the surviving spouse will inherit everything. But this is not true. Each state has its own laws about the way your money will be distributed if you die intestate. For example, in Oklahoma, if your husband died you would receive one half of your husband's entire estate. Any surviving children of your husband would receive the other half. You would receive the entire estate if your husband died and left neither parents, brother, sister, nor surviving children. If there are no surviving children, but a parent, brother, or sister of your husband's survives him, you, as the surviving spouse, would take all the marital property, plus an undivided one-third interest in the remaining estate. In Alaska, if your husband is survived by a parent you would inherit the first $50,000, plus one half the balance of the estate.

In a community-property state, you already own half the marital property. In California, if your husband died, you would inherit half of the marital property automatically as well as half of the community property of your husband. If there are no children, parents, sisters, or brothers, you would also receive all the separate property. If your husband leaves one child, you would receive only one half of the separate property. If your husband has more than one child, you would only receive one third of your husband's separate property. Your property would be treated the same way if you died first.

In ancient Rome, wills were read in public. If someone wanted to insult a despised enemy, he or she could put it in the will for all to hear.[1] Your will also becomes a public document; it is filed in the court system of your state.

A lot has been written about avoiding "probate" by not having a will. Probate really means "to prove" the will by having it approved in court. Avoiding probate gives you privacy. It also means eliminating probate fees, which vary from state to state. It does not, however, mean that you will avoid estate taxes that may be due.

Many people put all of their assets into what is called a "revocable living trust." This is a way to keep your assets out of the probate court. Assets in a living trust cannot be frozen for several months and can be managed without interruption. A living trust has a further advantage. If you become incapacitated, a successor trustee can easily manage your assets without the court appointing a guardian or a custodian. (A durable power of attorney can also be used to manage your assets easily without the court appointing a custodian.) However, putting all your assets in a living trust does entail legal fees. Avoiding probate does not mean you avoid estate taxes that may be due.

WHY HAVE A WILL?

Many couples think they do not need a will if everything is owned in joint name (as joint tenants with right of survivorship). This is true up to a point. But what happens if you both die in an accident? The laws of your state would then dictate how the money would be disbursed. You could also lose some tax benefits. (See Chapter 2 on advantages and disadvantages of joint ownership of property.) You and your husband may also think you do not need a will because you have property that will not be part of your estate—for example, insurance policies and retirement benefits that are paid directly to your beneficiaries and do not become part of your estate. Having a will allows for unlikely contingencies. You probably will not die with a winning lottery ticket in your pocket, but what if you do?

Many assets now pass outside people's wills because they are disposed of by contracts or other agreements. Having assets outside the will, by the way, does not mean the assets are not part of your estate for death tax purposes. If your husband, for example, has a business and an agreement to sell it should he die, he does not have to leave the business in his will. If you or your husband have a pension plan and have named beneficiaries, your pension plan is not named in your will. Only property that you own can be put in your will. If you and your husband own your house jointly, with a right of survivorship, you inherit the house if your husband dies first. His share of the house does not have to be left to you in his will, but if the house is in joint name, he can't leave his half to anyone else.

Wills let you give your property away as you wish. But only up to a point. Unless you have a prenuptial agreement that says you give up your inheritance rights to your husband's property, or he to yours, you must leave a certain amount to each other in all common law states except Georgia. This is known as the elective or forced share and is another holdover from our Anglo-Saxon traditions. In earlier times the husband would leave his wife the income from a portion of his land. More recently, the elective share could be satisfied by leaving the wife income from a trust, with assets usually not less than a third of the husband's probate estate.

Put simply, a husband or wife cannot disinherit a spouse who then might become a ward of the state. Each state has different rules for the so-called elective share. Your husband may have written a will before you were married and never revised his will to include you. If your husband dies and you discover that he wrote a will and left you out entirely, call a lawyer immediately. You usually have a limited time to file for your elective share. If your husband is very rich and left you very little, you may also be able to elect against the will. In some states the elective share is less than you would probably receive in a divorce settlement. New York's elective share law recently changed, allowing a wife or husband to claim an outright share instead of assets left in trust. In turn, your husband can claim a share of your estate, if you have cut him out.

Another important advantage to having a will is that it lets you name an executor—the person who is responsible for carrying out the terms of the will.

Moreover, a will is the place where you can name a guardian and make financial provisions for minor children. If you do not name a guardian, the court will appoint one for you. Many couples report that the naming of a guardian for young children is one of the biggest problems they face.

If you have children and die without a will, they may inherit money outright when they are eighteen in some states, twenty-one in others. Some children can deal with their newfound wealth; others do not do as well. Lawyers report seeing kids on great sprees and by twenty-five it is all gone, either on cars, boys or girls, or drugs.

A will is the place to disinherit your children, as well. State laws do not require that you leave a specific amount of money to your children. There is no forced share for children, except in Louisiana, where you must leave half your property to your children to be divided equally at your death. Lawyers advise that if you want to leave your children out, you must have a will to do this. You should make your intentions clear in case your child challenges your decision. Parents whose children have joined bizarre cults may want to be sure their hard-earned dollars do not end up supporting an ashram in India. While children do not automatically receive a share of the assets, if they are disinherited they are protected by various state laws if they are minors when you die.

If you are rich, a properly written will can help minimize federal estate taxes (which only begin on estates above $600,000 that are not left to a surviving spouse). States have different tax laws.

If you do not have a will and the court appoints an administrator, the estate may have to post a bond. Thus, having a will can save your estate unnecessary expenses.

Without a will it may take longer for the assets to be distributed.

A will also allows you to have the last word. When J. Paul Getty died, he left his villa in Italy to three of his girlfriends: One had the right to redecorate, one had the right to supervise the servants, and apparently all three had the right to live in it at the same time. Getty knew this would anger all three of the women.

Sometimes you might want to be sure a favorite, but not necessarily valuable, possession is in good hands. George Washington left "the gold-headed cane left me by Doctr. Franklin in his will" to his brother, Charles Washington. Washington's will also revealed him for the great statesman that he was. Unlike the legal language that is stuffed into the modern American will, rendering it basically indecipherable, Washington's handwritten document was clear and intelligent. In it he freed his slaves and, worried that some would not be able to support themselves, saw to it "that a regular and permanent fund be established for their support so long as there are subjects requiring it," and sought to establish a university in America so that "the youth of these United States" not be sent abroad where they were "contracting too frequently, not only habits of dissipation and extravagance, but principles unfriendly to Republican governm't and to the true and genuine liberties of mankind which thereafter are rarely overcome."[2]

Some lawyers advise, unless you have extremely valuable possessions, to list in a separate letter the personal property that you would like to give to friends or relatives.

This cuts down on legal costs and can avoid family arguments.

MEN WITHOUT WILL

Many men are reluctant to think about a will, let alone write one. Psychiatrists have long equated the reluctance to write a will with fear of death.[3] Pablo Picasso, who was ninety-one years old when he died on April 8, 1973, did not leave a will. In fact, he seems to have taken delight in predicting that the settling of his estate "will be worse than anyone imagines." The wrangling over his $260 million estate lasted almost four years. Eventually his assets were divided between his wife, his children, and his grandchildren. The government of France was given a large share of his paintings instead of death taxes. Lawyers fees consumed a huge chunk of the assets.[4]

Four U.S. presidents died without having written wills: Abraham Lincoln, Andrew Johnson, Ulysses S. Grant, and James A. Garfield.

Writing a will means having to admit one's mortality. It also means having to think about giving up control of one's assets. Some men are simply superstitious. They think writing a will will hasten their death. If a man's self-esteem is tied to his money, it is easy to understand that writing a will is anathema to him. A wealthy individual who leaves money in such a way that heirs can never gain control over it is probably quite different from the individual who leaves outright bequests to heirs. Sometimes men don't want to talk about a will because they then have to reveal how they value their property in relation to their wife and children. Recently, my friend Jane's husband, an advertising executive, died. Jane and Bill owned their home as tenants in common, which meant they could each name an heir for their share. When Bill died he left his half to his daughter from a previous marriage. His daughter wanted her money. So in addition to her grief, Jane had to sell her house. She also had to confront her anger at Bill. How could he have done this to her? Bill had felt that it was just a house. But Jane felt that it was her home.

For men there is an added problem. Those statistics that tell us that women will spend an average of fifteen years as widows are reminders to husbands that their wives will go on without them. Some men can contemplate this with reasonable humor; many cannot.

Surely Vincent Astor did. Mrs. Vincent Astor, speaking at a ceremony honoring her ninetieth birthday, recalled her husband telling her, "You're going to have a lot of fun with the foundation when I'm gone."[5] Mr. Astor was referring to the fact that his wife would, upon his death, become head of a foundation worth hundreds of millions of dollars. He felt that his wife would have an opportunity to use that money to good effect. And she has, becoming one of New York City's greatest philanthropists.

While you might suggest that your husband write a will, sometimes all of the reasons you can give are not enough to make your husband do it. One lawyer suggests that you should make an appointment to see the lawyer and then tell your husband the night before. Your husband may be waiting for just that little push.

Sometimes you can push too hard and then the will

won't count. At least that is what happened to Jean Gerard. Mrs. Gerard, a former ambassador to Luxembourg and a bigwig in the Republican party, inherited $10 million from her husband, James Gerard. There was only one problem: Gerard signed the will in his hospital bed only nine days before he died of bone cancer. In Gerard's previous will written four months earlier, he had left nothing outright to his wife but had left 40 percent of his assets in trust for her and the balance of his estate in trusts for his two children. After hearing thirty-five witnesses, the judge ruled that Mrs. Gerard had unduly influenced her husband, who was in no condition to think about such things.

Little has been written about women's attitude toward writing wills. One reason for this may be that women have seldom in the past made their own money. When they had money it was inherited, and usually left in such a way that the women had little control over how the money would be left after they died. Their husband's wills generally took care of passing the money on to the next generation. Today this is changing, and every woman should have a will to pass on her own assets to her husband and children and other heirs.

DEATH AND TAXES

While it's nice to know that your property will go where you want, the big reason people have wills is to keep their least favorite relative, Uncle Sam, from getting a penny more than he has to. Naturally, the more money you and your husband have, the more complicated this becomes.

You absolutely need a lawyer. The federal government plus your state government could claim a share of the money that you and your husband have saved, unless you have advice on the best way to take advantage of the current tax laws. Under current tax laws, only about six thousand estates each year owe any federal death taxes.

Since 1982 federal tax law permits a husband and wife to transfer to each other unlimited amounts of money without any taxes owed. (You must be a U.S. citizen to qualify for this transfer.) Before that, money left or given to a wife or husband above a certain amount was subject to an estate or gift tax. So if you and your husband have amassed a substantial amount of money, there are no taxes if you leave it all to each other when the first of you dies. But then that leaves the survivor with a large estate on which taxes would be owed, both to the federal and your state government.

If your combined net worth is less than $600,000 you do not have to worry. There will not be any taxes. If you are the survivor, one way to avoid any estate taxes would be to marry a younger man. You can then leave it all to him and no taxes would be due. This is not a plan most husbands will embrace with much enthusiasm.

Another way to avoid paying estate taxes is to give all your money away to charity. Or you can be like Charles Schwab. Charles Schwab was one of the great financiers of the twenties. Together with his partner, Andrew Carnegie, he founded the U.S. Steel Company. Andrew Carnegie left most of his money to a variety of philanthropic causes. Schwab, who died nearly broke in 1939, said, "I disagreed with Carnegie's ideas on how best to distribute his wealth. I spent mine."

While we can each leave unlimited amounts of money to our husbands, and they to us, without paying any taxes whatsoever, if we leave money to anyone else—to our children, other relatives, or friends—the federal government wants a share of any money you leave above your lifetime exemption of $600,000. If, therefore, you and your husband were to leave everything you owned to each other, no taxes are due. If you die first, no taxes will be owed on any money you leave your husband. If your husband dies first, there is no tax on the money he leaves you. The problem comes with what lawyers call "the second to die." Assuming you haven't remarried, if there is more than $600,000 there will be taxes to pay. Estate taxes begin at 37 percent and move up to 55 percent on estates of $3 million, rising to 60 percent for transfers between $10 and $21 million. The time to plan for avoiding some of these taxes is before either one of you dies.

Avoiding the tax on that $600,000 is known as estate planning. There are several ways to do it. The one I like best is to equalize your assets. If you and your husband each have $600,000, you can each leave your heirs $600,000 without incurring any estate taxes. If all of your assets are in your husband's name and you die first, your $600,000 exemption is lost. If your husband doesn't re-marry and dies with an estate of $1.2 million, he can only leave $600,000 tax free—a heavy tax will be due on the second $600,000. In other words, if either of you dies with the entire $1.2 million in your estate you will have to pay estate taxes. Each of you should create a marital trust into which you put $600,000. Your husband names you the beneficiary of his trust: You have all the income and when you die the trust then goes to your children. You do the same thing with your $600,000.

While owning all of your property in joint name is highly desirable and epitomizes the sharing aspects of marriage, it could mean that the spouse who dies first will lose the $600,000 exemption.

Federal tax laws offer another option for reducing estate taxes. Each of us can give $10,000, or for a couple $20,000, to as many people as we would like, each year, without incurring any gift taxes. If you have two kids and three grandchildren, you can kick $100,000 a year out of your estate each year. That way, you can keep your assets down to the $600,000. All good, but sometimes you can worry too much about taxes. The money you give to your children could be needed to take care of illnesses in your old age, or could give you and your husband a chance to take trips and enjoy extras.

Another way to take money out of your estate is to pay for your grandchildren's college education. If you pay the tuition directly to the school, you do not have to pay a gift tax. This is in addition to the $10,000 a year you can give each child without gift taxes.

DIFFERENT WILLS FOR DIFFERENT TIMES

A good will is the best way you and your husband can protect each other and your children when death comes. Unlike prenuptial agreements and divorces, most wills are not areas of major battle. If you and your husband discuss and make financial decisions together, it is more than likely that you will discuss wills. If you and your husband contribute to the family income, it is important that each of you knows how you will manage without that income.

If you are a woman who has never handled the family

finances, your husband may think he is protecting you by keeping you in the dark about his plans and leaving everything in the hands of a trustee. This really isn't fair to you. The husband who says "If anything happens to me, just call Fred, the accountant," may not realize that you would prefer to know what will happen to you ahead of time. You should know. You should ask. One lawyer reports, "After a widow goes through a mourning process [she] blooms. They start out doubting their own capabilities. They end up being competent and even enjoy handling their own finances." Think about Katharine Graham. She inherited *The Washington Post* from her husband when he died in 1963. Mrs. Graham, a housewife, took over. She said, "I quickly learned that things don't stand still—you have to make decisions." She made enough of the right ones to make her family one of America's wealthiest, with an estimated net worth of $580 million.[6]

Wills play a slightly different role in second marriages. Many couples, especially if they have children from first marriages, want prenuptial agreements in order to be sure that money will go to their children from a first marriage. If your husband is leaving money in trust—where you get the interest and his children get the principal—conflicts can easily develop. Sometimes you don't need a second marriage for that to happen. One widow tells of wanting to buy a condominium in Florida to spend time there with her second husband. Her children were enraged that she was spending what they considered their money on another man.

If it's a second marriage and you and your husband have old wills that left assets to your previous mates, divorce usually automatically cancels out the first wife or husband in a previously written will—but not always. In Iowa, for example, if a will refers to a former wife by her name, Jane Smith, but not as "my wife, Jane Smith," the will would stand despite a divorce. And in Louisiana and Mississippi, divorce does not automatically revoke a will. So if you or your husband had wills when you were previously married to others, be sure to change them.

Wills are probably one of the last bastions of tradition, written by lawyers who were educated under old laws and with old attitudes that continue to assume that a woman must be protected, that a woman must have money doled out to her. Not infrequently, men write wills that give control of family businesses to their sons, while leaving money in trust for their wives and daughters.

TRUST ME

Frequently, in common law states, assets are owned by the husband. He consults a lawyer. The lawyer urges him to write a will that protects the money more than it protects his wife. Typically this involves leaving the money in a trust. Unfortunately, the planning that gives the least amount of money to the government also sometimes gives you, the widow, the least amount of control over the money. The planning starts with a careful calculation of your net worth and your husband's, as well as a look at the way in which property is owned jointly, separately, in common, etc.

Here's how it was described in one recently published book:

Ned's plan had been carefully prepared, but he had made one major miscalculation. When left on her own, Ned's wife proved to be a very poor manager of money. Between her grief at having become a widow at such a young age and her lack of familiarity with the specifics of investments Ned's estate was wiped out within a few short years.[7]

The message is implicit: Women are incapable; do not leave them money outright. It is a message that seems to pervade the legal profession as well as the estate-planning contingent. And the best way not to leave money directly to your wife, child, or husband is by leaving money in trust.

Trusts are, as far as I am concerned, a misnomer. My dictionary defines *trust* as complete assurance, faith, and dependence. But there is also a submeaning of guarding and preserving. This definition is generally applied to trusts.

Trusts are great in certain situations. If you and your husband die in an accident, you would certainly want money left in trust for your minor children.

If you or your husband have elderly parents, you might want to establish trusts to take care of them in the event that something would happen to either of you. Trusts are not as advisable until you have assets of at least $600,000 each. If you and your husband are young, leaving money to each other in trust may not make sense. Why lock up the money for years?

You can establish a trust while you are alive. This is called an inter vivos trust. A trust that is established after you die is called a testamentary trust. Trusts are revocable or irrevocable. There are usually tax advantages to an irrevocable trust, but not to a revocable trust. While you are alive, you might want revocable trusts in case you change your mind about the trustee.

When you die your executor is responsible for setting up any testamentary trusts called for by your will. The trust then becomes a separate legal entity that pays taxes. Our tax laws make the trust an attractive way to leave money. The more money you and your husband have accumulated, the more likely your wills will include various trusts. Here are some of the current favorites:

First of all, there is the QTIP trust—the Qualified Terminable Interest Property trust. This trust seems to have been custom-made for the controlling husband. It is also ideal for second marriages. Your husband puts his money in trust. You the wife are allowed some income, but the ultimate beneficiaries of the trust are decided by your husband in his will. You are, in effect, treated like a child on an allowance.

Lawyers love this one, especially when they are named as trustees and can collect a fee for doling out the income to you.

The bypass trust (also called a credit shelter trust) is another estate planners' favorite. Your husband, who controls the assets, puts $600,000—his lifetime exemption—into a bypass trust. You can get the income and the trustee can also have the power to give you principal from the trust. The rest of your husband's money can be yours tax free because of the unlimited marital deduction.

There is also the classic marital deduction trust, not much used since the creation of QTIPs. Here's how this one works, as described in a financial planning book: The "surviving spouse is provided with income for life and the power to appoint who will receive the trust principal. There's lots of flexibility regarding the powers of the trustee to withdraw principal or even for the surviving spouse to withdraw principal." The part I like is the following: "The big feature of the classic marital trust is that the management of the fund is taken out of the spouse's hands. A surviving spouse can be protected from the manipulations of children and relatives because control ultimately rests with the trustee."[8] Notice the gender-neutral language. But the implication is clear: Keep the money out of the hands of the little woman. The irony here is that when the wife dies her trust will usually go to her children or her husband's children from a previous marriage—outright—even if the children are only in their early twenties.

Tax experts have also figured out how you can have your money and give it away to charity as well. There are several types of charitable trusts that can help. The main idea is that you can get a tax deduction for giving assets to a charity while at the same time retaining some of the income for you or your heirs.

Charitable Lead Trust: You establish a trust with a fixed sum of money and receive a tax deduction for a portion of the contributed amount. The money produces income. That income goes to the charity for a fixed number of years. At the end of the fixed period the trust goes back to the beneficiary, either you, the donor, or your heirs. In other words, you get a tax deduction and then get your money back.

Charitable Remainder Trust: This is almost the opposite of the charitable lead trust. You or your husband establish a trust, you get the income, then when you die, the charity you designate gets the remainder. Jacqueline

Onassis's will set up a charitable remainder trust. Her grandchildren will inherit the remainder in twenty-four years. Many public charities offer donors ways to donate money through such trusts. In one type of trust, the charitable remainder annuity trust, the donor knows ahead of time the rate of income that will be generated. In another type, the charitable remainder unitrust, the payout fluctuates.

The drawback to such trusts is that they are irrevocable.[9]

So what should you do? Know as much as possible about your family finances. Discuss your intentions and your husband's. If your husband can't think about writing a will, make the appointment with the lawyer yourself, then tell your husband what you've done. He'll probably go with you. Above all, discuss possible trustees with your husband if either of you plans to establish trusts. Trustees can wield great power. There's a reason for all those cartoons about bank trust departments and weeping widows.

TRUSTS AND HOW THEY WORK

A *trust* is an arrangement in which someone holds assets for the benefit of someone else.

The *grantor* is the person who sets up the trust (also called the settlor, the donor, the creator, or the trustor).

The *beneficiary* is the person, or persons, who receives the economic benefits. There are two types:

The *income beneficiary* is the person who gets the income (frequently the wife, especially with older husbands).

The *ultimate beneficiary,* also called the remainder

beneficiary, is the person, or persons, who gets the assets of the trust when the trust ends (frequently your children or a designated charity).

The *trustee* is the person, or institution, who has legal title to the assets that are in the trust.

The most important of the above for you to understand is the trustee. The trustee must carry out the obligations set forth in the trust agreement—such as managing the assets by investing them, paying out the income, running a business, or paying the necessary taxes. Choosing a trustee is crucial if you plan to leave money in trust for your children, your parents, or your husband. It's also important if your husband plans to leave money in trust for you.

The trustee is the person who manages the trust. Trustees are paid for doing this. The fee varies depending on the size of the trust and its complexity. If you are planning to establish a trust in your will or your husband in his, you can establish the fee before you write the trust. The person who establishes the trust can give the trustee broad or narrow powers. If you give the trustee broad powers you want to be sure the trustee is somebody with good judgment.

There are two types of trustees: the professional trustee, from a law firm or bank trust department, or the trusted friend. My own preference would be for the trusted friend. The professional trustee—the lawyer or banker—will usually try to suggest that the bank or the law firm will be there long after your trusted friend is gone. The number of banks and law firms that have either merged or failed over the past few years makes that argument somewhat less forceful than it used to be. Furthermore, when you appoint a bank as a trustee, you can never be sure who in the bank will actually manage your trust. It could be a recent MBA graduate learning the ropes on your trust, or it could be a venerable old gentleman who never made it out of the trust department.

A capable friend who acts as trustee has a big advantage over the bank trust department named in a will. The friend trustee can pick and choose how the trust should be invested and can change investment advisors should the performance be less than satisfactory. If a trust is locked into a bank trust department you have little chance to make a change.

You have to be careful not to pick a trustee who will love the control. You also have to understand the possible conflict a trustee has. If you have a trust with $1 million in it and the trustee is paid a 1 percent fee for managing it, that means the trustee earns $10,000 a year. If you, the wife, would like to yank a few hundred thousand dollars out of your trust to buy an apartment, the trustee may decide it is not a good idea—after all, the trustee's fee will drop if the assets diminish.

There is another problem with trusts that should be pointed out. Most of the time trusts are supposed to pay out the income. That's very good if trust assets are invested in CDs paying 9 percent. But it is not very good if they are invested in CDs that only yield 5 percent. You would suddenly have a big drop in income. Trusts must allow for this kind of shift and therefore must be flexible in the way they invest as well as in the way they pay out money. The trustee should have some idea that the donor of the trust, your husband, would rather see the trust diminish and have you maintain your standard of living.

There are many ways to leave money, but trying to be too restrictive for too long can result in unexpected consequences.

A trust agreement that is too rigid could turn out to be a disaster. In one case, a man set up a trust and his wife was to receive only the interest. The balance was to go to charity when he died. His wife outlived him by thirty years. Inflation totally eroded the buying power of her income and she had to spend her old age living on very little.

A big question is: Should you name your husband as a trustee and should he name you? Were there no tax implications, the answer would be easy. Name your husband; ask your husband to name you as trustee. You should also name a co-trustee and a successor trustee. It doesn't matter that you may not know how to invest money. Nobody will be more concerned about hiring good money managers for your money than you. If you don't know, you will learn. My first husband never had a will until I refused to travel with him unless we both made wills to name a guardian for our daughter. Then the unlikely happened. My husband drowned while on a fishing trip leaving me alone with our one-year-old daughter. His will named me as one of his executors. My husband's will also established a trust and named me and one of his business partners as trustees. It was a decision for which I will always be grateful. Having a friend, instead of a bank or lawyer whom I hardly knew, at a time when I was so devastated meant a great deal to me. As an executor and trustee I also had to make decisions. This sense of being in control helped me gradually to rebuild my own shattered life.

Tax implications are important in the naming of trustees. One of the main purposes of setting up certain trusts is to avoid having to pay estate taxes. But there's a catch. For example, if you, the wife, were the trustee of a credit shelter trust and had the power to invade the trust, the tax advantage would be lost.

THINGS TO KNOW BEFORE WRITING A WILL

You and your husband will have to decide about executors for your wills. The executor's role is slightly different from that of the trustee's. The executor is really the stage manager for your estate. (The estate, by the way, is everything you left behind.) The basic job of the executor is to carry out the instructions in your will. While this calls for many technical and legal responsibilities, you do not have to name a lawyer or a professional for the job. If you become the executor you can hire a lawyer to do the work. Executors are paid fees based on a percentage of the assets of the estate. In California, executors' fees are set by statutes: 4.9 percent of the first $15 thousand, 3 percent of the next $85 thousand, 2 percent of the next $900 thousand, 1 percent of the next $9 million, .5 percent of the next $15 million. Above that, the court decides. Lawyers can be hired to do the specific tasks for a lot less, in some cases. If you serve as executor you are entitled to that fee. However, if you receive an executor's fee, it is taxable income for you.

The executor files the will for probate, pays any debts that are due, pays the funeral expenses, and lists the assets and liabilities. (This is the kind of information you and your husband should already have.)

The executor also must file the federal and state death

tax returns. The federal estate tax return is due nine months after the date of death, regardless of whether any taxes are owed, although extensions are possible.

As with trustees you can name a close friend or a professional institution. If you do name a friend, be sure to tell the friend. Being an executor is time consuming and not everyone wants to take on the job. Be careful about naming a bank, which may only take an estate of a minimum size.

The best choice of an executor is probably your husband for your will and you for your husband's will. You might also consider a coexecutor for large estates. Usually you would also name a successor executor. You can also spell out fees for executors in your will that will override state laws. Be sure the potential executors agree in advance.

WHAT YOU SHOULD KNOW ABOUT YOUR HUSBAND'S WILL

Here are six basic things you should know:

1. Where it is
2. If there is a trust, what type of trust and what its terms are
3. What happens to the trust
4. What, if anything, is left for the children
5. Who the trustees are
6. Who the executors are

While these are the things that will be part of the will, there is other information that you should also know:

What taxes, if any, will be due to Uncle Sam and to the state and when will they be due? The death of your husband does not mean Uncle Sam does not claim income taxes that were due on any income earned up until the day your husband died.

If your husband's assets are mainly real estate and not left only to you, you should find out whether you will have to sell property in order to pay the estate taxes. There are some provisions for extending the time frame for making these payments. Another way not to have to force the sale of property in order to pay the taxes is to create an insurance trust. If your husband has insurance, but he is the owner of that insurance, it goes into his estate and taxes are due. If a trust owns the insurance and is the beneficiary, the money goes to the trust; there are no taxes due. The insurance money can be used to pay estate taxes. This is very important if you want to avoid selling a property or a family business.

If your husband runs his own business, will you know what to do to keep it running? Will you be able to meet the immediate payroll? Is there someone who can step in to take over, and have you discussed this with your husband? If you and your husband are in business together or the business is yours, there are several routes to take. If it's your business or your husband's and you have partners, you could have a buy-sell agreement. This usually establishes a fixed price at which one of you buys out the other. If your husband has a buy-sell agreement, you should know about it. The big problem here is not revaluing the business. You could end up having your husband's share bought out by his partners, at a price that was established years ago, while the business has continued to grow. Or, worse still, you might have to buy out a partner at an overvalued price that was established when things were going well, but since then the business has collapsed.

Frequently, the way to provide for buying out a partner in such a situation is with an insurance trust.

You might have a family business that you would like to keep in the family. There are ways to do that, too. The usual way is to give your children stock when the business is just beginning. That way they become owners at low cost. If the children are very young, the stock is put into trust.

There is yet another method called the estate freeze. This is complicated, tricky, and requires the advice of highly specialized experts. It involves two classes of stock. One class appreciates in value, the other has a value that is fixed, or frozen. You or your husband keep the frozen-value stock and give the stock that appreciates to your children.

While all of this may seem remote, especially if you are young, believe me—this can happen to anyone. Knowing a little about your situation can take away the anxiety and fear that you will be unable to manage.

If despite everything you and your husband refuse to write wills, all is not totally lost—well, at least to some extent. There is a little lawyer's trick known as post-mortem tax planning. Suppose your husband forgot to write a will. You inherit everything. Your husband's $600,000 exemption is lost, ordinarily. But you can "disclaim" an amount up to $600,000 and let it go directly to your children. It's risky, however, because not all states allow a disclaimer, especially for jointly owned property.

What If You Were Suddenly Widowed?

Here's a list of questions you and your husband might try and answer. You will probably think of many more.

1. How would you meet the monthly expenses that are now paid by your husband's income and your income? Most couples cover this gap by having life insurance—term insurance when you are young, whole life when you get older.
2. Would you have cash for funeral expenses? Here's where a separate account that can't be frozen is helpful. Funeral expenses vary but on average can be $3,000.
3. If you are insured under your husband's health plan, could you continue it? Most companies give you thirty-six months in which you can continue to pay for coverage. During that time you should find out whether you will be able to convert the policy to keep it on your own or can find another insurer. Don't forget to ask; the company may not call to tell you.
4. Would you be eligible for Social Security benefits? You would be if your husband was covered. You can get widow's benefits as well as benefits for your children. The trouble here is that the benefits stop when your children are sixteen. Then you are not eligible for benefits again until you are sixty-two, when you can get retirement benefits. But if you begin drawing benefits at age sixty-two you will receive a lower amount than if you wait until you are sixty-five. If you remarry before age sixty, you lose the right to widow's benefits;

marry after sixty and you keep your benefits and your new husband.

5. Would you be able to continue living in your house? Frequently couples have mortgage insurance that pays off the house if the husband dies. This may not be the best way to insure your house. You would be better off having life insurance for the amount of the mortgage. Coverage would be cheaper. In addition, the insurance would go directly to you, and you could continue the mortgage payments. You would have more control over making a decision about your house than if the mortgage were automatically paid.

6. How would you pay for your children's education?

7. What if you have a lot of debts?

These are hard questions to think about, let alone plan for. If you and your husband do nothing else, you should at least know the basics—where your assets are, how they are owned, and how much of them will be yours, should something happen to him. If he has lawyers, brokers, or other advisers get to know them too. The main point should be that you end up with as much control over your assets as possible, and feel comfortable managing them.

A GUIDE TO BEING ALONE

If your husband dies you are a widow. The word comes from the old English. In addition to its primary meaning as a woman who has lost her husband, the word is defined as "empty" or "extra hand at the card table." Unfortunately, that is also the way many people, even friends, will sometimes regard you once you are no longer part of a couple. The implication that "widow" conjures up for many people is deeply rooted in earlier times. Then, and even today, widows were often entitled only to their "dower" rights. This generally meant the "income" from a part of their husbands' estates.

WHEN THE TIME COMES

I can tell you that nothing in life prepares you for the trauma of losing your husband. Nevertheless you should try to plan the funeral. This is not one of life's easier tasks. Remember, an expensive service is probably not the best use of your money, especially if you are uncertain of your future finances. Your local funeral director will be able to tell you the proper procedures. But you can have whatever touches you would like. My husband and I recently attended a service where a favorite shawl was draped over the casket of the friend who had died. It was a simple and lovely gesture, and a very personal reminder of our friend. Costs average around $3,000. Much depends on the elaborateness of the casket you choose and the number of cars you rent for the cemetery. Flowers are another consideration. You may also want to place a notice in your local newspaper. The clergyman is generally paid a small amount, in cash.

Some people choose to plan funerals in advance. There are even prepaid plans. If you want to do this, here are a few tips: You can check prices at a few funeral homes before making a decision. You can even have a trust where your money will accumulate, until needed, and earn interest. Here you have to be careful as to what happens to any excess money. In some states, that money could go to the funeral director. You also have to be sure that inflation is figured into your plan so that there will be no extra charges.

During the First Month

Find the will. If there is a will, it will have to be probated. While you can go through the probate process alone if you are the executor, you are probably better off hiring a lawyer.

There is more than one kind of probate and the process differs in each state. Some states have a special small-estate process when the total estate is a maximum ranging anywhere from $2,000 to as much as $100,000. Probate does not have to be done immediately, but it should be done in the first few weeks. The ultimate goal of probate is to be sure debts are paid and heirs get what they should.

During the First Three Months

You will also need copies of the death certificate; in some cases these must be certified. You may need as many as twelve. The funeral director can help you with this. You need the certificates in order to collect life insurance and anything else for which you may be the beneficiary. You also need it to transfer assets to your name, to probate a will, and for other purposes as well.

Here is a list of items that will need to be transferred into your name:

- Title to your house, if it was jointly owned
- Bank accounts—Joint accounts could be frozen, which is one reason you should have an account in your own name.
- Credit cards—If you have credit cards in your own name you can continue to use them. If your credit cards are all in your husband's name, and you signed on them, you can probably continue to use them. As long as you continue to pay on time, you will not have any problems. But at some point you will probably want to notify the company and have the cards changed to your name. Be sure you have records to document that you were an authorized signer. If you had a joint credit card, notify the company that the card should be in your name only.
- Automobile title
- Auto insurance
- Securities

You should also review your will. If your husband was the executor, you will need to name somebody else. Sign a durable power of attorney. Sign a health-care power of attorney. (Actually, you and your husband should both have them.)

If your husband was the beneficiary of your pension or life insurance, change this.

If your husband worked with lawyers, accountants, or other advisers, meet with them. Decide whether you want to continue working with them. You don't have to. Even if it is the lawyer who drew his will, you can hire your own.

If you were working, go back to work, not only for the

income, but because having something to do every day will lessen some of your grief.

Take a look at your finances during the first three months and redo your net worth (asset and liability) statement as well as your cash-flow statement. (See pages 34–35 and 36–37.)

Review your insurance needs. If you have young children, you may need life insurance. If you are working, you may need disability insurance. If your husband was the beneficiary of your life insurance, you may not need it anymore.

Social Security: You are eligible to collect if your husband had paid into Social Security and you are a surviving spouse with minor children. As noted earlier, you and your children can collect benefits until the children reach sixteen. Then all benefits to you stop unless you are at least sixty-two years old. You are also eligible to collect as a widow, without children, when you reach the age of sixty-two. You will receive benefits based on either your own earnings or your husband's, whichever is higher. If you and your husband were already collecting benefits, you will have to notify the Social Security office of his death. You will continue to receive benefits, but they will decrease. The toll-free number for Social Security is 1(800)772-1213. Documentation you will require:

- Your husband's Social Security number
- Your Social Security number
- Your children's Social Security numbers if they are minor children
- Your children's birth certificates
- Your marriage certificate

• Your husband's W-2 form or a federal self-employment tax return for the most recent year

Life insurance: Notify the insurance company, either directly or through your insurance agent. The named beneficiary is paid directly, usually in two to three weeks. You will need a death certificate.

Pensions: If you and your husband were receiving pension benefits under his pension and it was a single annuity, your benefits will stop. If you and your husband were receiving benefits from your husband's pension and it was a joint and survivor plan, the amount might change depending on the type of benefits you were receiving. If your husband was not yet retired, notify his employer and find out about any lump-sum payouts that may be due to you.

Investments: If you are unfamiliar with your husband's investments, call the broker and have the statements sent to you. Then ask the broker to explain the reasons various stocks and bonds were chosen by your husband. If your husband always invested your money, and you suddenly find that you have received the proceeds from his life insurance in a lump sum, immediately put the money into a money market fund. Don't even think about doing anything else—no matter who recommends it. It's your money now. You will have plenty of time later to decide how to invest. If you are getting pension proceeds or life insurance in a lump sum, you will possibly have to make a choice as to how to invest this money. One possibility is an annuity. While annuities can offer a certain amount of safety in the short run, they are usually paid out in fixed sums, so are less likely to keep pace with inflation. In addition, you give up control over your money.

Debts: Usually a notice placed in the local newspaper announces the death so that anyone with outstanding claims can come forward. A specific number of days is usually allowed in which claims may be filed. If debts were in his name only, the executor must pay them. If they were in joint name, you may have to pay them.

Medical Insurance: If your husband was working and had medical insurance, call the company to find out about continuing the policy to extend to you and your family. Under COBRA laws, you must be given the chance to continue the policy for thirty-six months. After that you may be able to get a conversion policy. Find out if you will have to requalify for the conversion policy.

Estate taxes: There are no federal taxes if money is left just to you. Taxes are owed, however, on amounts that exceed $600,000 left to other beneficiaries. Many states have inheritance or estate taxes. Most states have no taxes beyond the amount the federal government allows as a credit against federal estate-tax payments.

Income taxes: You will have to file a return as usual, and can continue to file a joint return for the year in which your husband died. If you have dependent children, you can file a joint return for two years. If money is being paid to you from an annuity, you must pay income tax on it.

What Not to Do

1. Do not make decisions about selling your house, unless this is something you and your husband carefully planned.

2. Do not buy anything from anybody that the seller claims will give you an income for life.

During the First Year

Think about whether you want to keep your house. This should not just be based on economics, but on your feelings as well.

The finances are easy to calculate. You have to decide, if your income is less than when you were married, if you are making a sacrifice out of some loyalty to the marital home or to your children who do not want you to sell.

Keep in mind how the taxation works when you inherit the house, providing you did not own it outright but received it as either half of a joint tenancy with your husband or inherited it from your husband. You inherit your husband's part of the house—either his half or the entire house at what is called the "stepped-up" basis in value. No taxes are due when you inherit the house. Taxes would be due if you decided to sell the house. That's when cost basis counts.

Here's an example:

Original cost of the house:	$100,000
Value of the house when your husband dies:	$250,000
Your basis if your husband owned the house:	$250,000

If you sold the house for $250,000 there would not be a capital-gains tax. Your basis if you owned the house jointly would be:

Your half:	$ 50,000
His half:	$125,000
Your new basis:	$175,000

If the house was owned jointly and you sold it for $250,000 you would have a taxable profit of $75,000. If you are fifty-five or over you would have a onetime exclusion of $125,000 so you would not have a tax. If you had rolled over gains from a previous sale, your basis would be reduced by the amount of the earlier gain.

You have to decide whether you will do better with a smaller house and some income from the proceeds of your sale. If you decide to sell and have anything of value—say, worth over $1,000—you might want to consult a dealer or an auction house. Otherwise, you might want to have a tag sale to reduce the accumulation of several years that you would otherwise have to cart away with you.

Special Advice for Older Women

You want to be sure that you will be all right should you become ill and incapacitated in your old age. Many of my friends have parents who are now getting old. The situation is often the same—everything is fine until the father dies and the mother is alone. The mother is fine for the first few years. Then many begin to fail. Sometimes it is her health, sometimes her mind. One friend's mother, living alone in a Florida condominium, began to imagine that people were trying to break into her apartment. My friend and her two sisters pooled their money and bought a small house that one sister and her husband lived in with the mother. This worked for a while, but eventually the mother needed the care of a nursing home. If you have children, discuss the possibilities with them of what might happen to you and how you would like things handled.

Here are a few things to consider:

- Possibly buying into a retirement community
- Selling your house while you still have the energy to move and the house has not gotten to be too much of a burden to you
- Making funeral arrangements—One woman I know even purchased her own casket because, she said, if she left it to her son, an artist, he would try and build one and she might never be buried.

If you do not have children, or feel that they are too far away to be of help should you have problems, find an elder-care attorney with whom you can discuss your future. Check on the elder care services in your community. You may want to consider giving away some of your assets in order to qualify for nursing home care. You may want to consider nursing home insurance. If you are managing your own assets, you may want to put them in a living trust to make it easier for someone else to take over, or else sign a durable power of attorney. A power of attorney is an appointment to let someone else act for you. A durable power of attorney lets someone else act for you even if you become incapacitated. A springing power of attorney is only activated if you become incapacitated.

Many women who are alone and faced for the first time with having to handle their own money seem to make some of the same mistakes.

The Five Most Common Mistakes Made by Women Whose Husbands Always Did Everything for Them

1. Thinking if her husband did it a particular way, it must be right. An example is the woman who inherited a

portfolio of CDs that had been yielding 9 percent. When yields dropped, she refused to change her husband's plan.

2. Being unwilling to take any investment risk. By not taking any risk a woman's investments do not keep pace with inflation and she keeps having to reduce her expenses because her dollars buy less and less. Your money has to generate increasing, not diminishing, income.

3. Giving loans to her children. This leaves her with even less money, thus making her more fearful and unable to manage. Often, women left alone after long marriages feel life is not going to offer much anymore, or they feel guilty for surviving, and are therefore vulnerable to requests from their children, who frequently promise to pay back, but often have problems doing so. Resist the temptation.

4. Meeting a new man and letting him take charge because she feels she cannot handle money. Most women can, and should, handle their own investments—if not on a daily basis, at least by frequently consulting a broker or advisor.

5. Being unable to understand the reality of her new situation and thus failing to cut expenses. An example of what can happen is a couple where the husband's income had been $75,000. The wife didn't work. After her husband died she was left with assets of $250,000. Her income dropped to below $25,000. This was a drastic change, which she could not accept.

Many women have been faced with the same problems, although each person's situation is different. The more knowledge you have beforehand, the better equipped you will be. But even if you are starting out with little awareness, you can learn quickly. One woman said she learned the most by asking her friends. She never asked for general advice. She always asked for specific information. If one friend knew about automobiles, she asked that friend about cars. If another friend knew about insurance, she would address her insurance questions to that friend. You may not have such competent friends, but you can do a lot of your own research, and you can learn.

9.
Cinderella Revised: The Rights of Children

We all know the story of Cinderella. While modern writers have accused women of having a Cinderella complex—waiting for their prince to rescue them— few people seem to have concentrated on the real villain: not the wicked stepmother, but the wicked father. Haven't you wondered what kind of man would allow a woman into his life who would do such terrible things to his children? Haven't you wondered why his right to do this is never questioned?

CHILD'S RITES

Children's rights have changed dramatically over the centuries. In ancient Rome, children were raised at the whim of the father. When the child was born, the father could either keep the baby or order that it be left exposed to the elements. When a baby was born the midwife placed the child on the ground. The father could either lift up the child, signifying his intention of raising the child, or leave it on the ground to die. Often children were left to die in order to preserve intact the inheritance of the children already living. They were also frequently given up for adoption, particularly when the natural parents could not afford to give the child advantages. Octavius, who became the emperor Augustus, was the adopted son of Julius Caesar. Children were used in order to form political alliances, make advantageous marriages, or to serve the aims of their parents in other ways.[1]

Roman sons remained subject to their fathers' rule until the fathers died. (Roman women were under the thumb of first their fathers and then their husbands.) The earnings of the son belonged to the father, and fathers could disinherit their sons. And since Roman women often died in childbirth, a stepmother who could influence the father could prove to be a great threat to the children of a first marriage.

Americans have moved a long way from pagan Rome. The rights of children are increasingly protected by federal and state laws. The official definition of *child* is a person who has not reached the age of majority, usually eighteen, who is not married, and is still at home. American children have specific rights. Children are, at least theoretically, protected from the abuse of parents. This means a court order can remove children from a home where abuse is suspected. After "emancipation" parents are no longer responsible for their children, although in some states parents are responsible for their disabled children, even after the age of emancipation.

Unlike the Romans, Americans have long believed in the maternal right. Until fairly recently, mothers were awarded custody of their children unless there was an extremely unusual circumstance. Fathers paid support in the event of divorce. In the last few decades, however, fathers, claiming equal rights, have begun to seek custody of their children.[2] The increasing number of stepparents has further complicated the idea of custody, throwing doubt into the once-sacred doctrine that the "natural parent" should raise a child. One example is the child who was raised by a mother and stepfather. In the past, if the mother died, the natural father would automatically be given custody of the child, even if he had previously abandoned that child. Today, the best interests of the child are considered, and custody might be awarded to the stepfather who had raised the child.[3]

Children have the right to make contracts with adults, and to have these contracts enforced. On the other hand, children cannot have contracts with adults enforced against them.

American parents also have certain legal obligations toward their children. Children are entitled to support and education. Children also have the right to medical care. Sometimes this right is enforced by courts when the religious beliefs of parents may prohibit medical intervention.

The money that children earn or inherit is also protected. An example might be a child actress who earns a high salary. Her salary must be used only for her support. In one situation, the mother of a young actress became ill and had no health insurance. The mother, who had guided her daughter's career, could not use any of her daughter's money for medical expenses, even though the daughter would have wanted to help her mother. Parents must consider themselves guardians of the money. Occasionally, children have sued parents and accused them of mismanaging funds left for them.

If you and your husband die intestate, your children have certain rights to inherit money from your estates. However, except in Louisiana, you do not have to leave money to your children.

Should you or your husband die, your children may also be eligible to receive survivors' benefits from Social Security. If your husband died and he had paid into Social Security, your children would be entitled to benefits from the time your husband died until they reach the age of eighteen. They would be able to receive benefits until they are nineteen if they are full-time high school students. The benefits would be based on your husband's benefits. Your children would also be entitled to benefits based on your Social Security if you died.

If you or your husband retire and are entitled to receive Social Security benefits, your children may also be entitled to benefits under special circumstances—if they are under age eighteen, or if they are over eighteen and disabled. If you or your husband retire and are entitled to a maximum benefit, each of your children can receive up to half of your benefit. (The government does draw the line, however, with something known as Family Limits.)

MOTHERHOOD

Should you and your husband divorce, the law becomes quite specific about your obligations to your children. Child support and child custody are carefully spelled out in divorce and separation agreements. However, during marriage parents must make their own rules about how to raise their children.

For many couples, the decision to have children is the most important decision they will make. The decision may be even more critical for many women than for men. No matter how equally a couple may decide to divide marital obligations and no matter how willing the father is to help, it is still the mother who must physically give birth to the child. The mother is also most often the person who remains responsible for that child. More often than not it is the mother who cuts back on her career and forfeits some of her earlier goals in order to take care of her child. And, should the marriage end in divorce, mothers, not fathers, end up with custody and responsibility for the children.

CHILD SUPPORT IN DIVORCE

While the law in general says children are entitled to support, when a couple divorces, laws become much more specific about a child's rights. Since 1984, all states have been required to have specific child-support guidelines. Basically, these guidelines consider the income of the parents and the standard of living that the income of the parents should afford the children. Often the support guidelines are some percentage of the gross income of the noncustodial parent, or else a percentage of the combined incomes of both parents. The different methods of computing child support can lead to a big difference in the type of award the custodial parent will be given.[4]

One problem with child-support awards is the nonmonetary costs—usually borne by the mother. Studies estimate that divorced mothers spend between 19.6 and 26.6 hours each week taking care of their children. If a monetary value is put on that time, studies have come up with a figure of $123,553 as the nonmonetary cost of caring for a child until the age of eighteen.[5]

So much for the theory. In practice, fathers frequently underreport income when awards are made, and then fail to pay the necessary support after the divorce. In some situations, no child support is awarded at all. In a recent study of 670 Connecticut divorces, no support was ordered in 20 percent of the families studied. The average weekly support ordered for each child was $49.58. A further Connecticut study reported that 82 percent of the mothers were awarded sole custody of their children, yet 26 percent reported that the fathers were not paying the ordered support.[6] Nationally, uncollected payments of $19 billion have been estimated.[7] According to a 1989 Census Bureau study, only half of the 5 million women entitled to child support received it in full.[8] On the other hand, there are fathers who go the other way, using their time with the children to lavish material goods on them. Often when parents divorce, mothers find that they must struggle on a limited budget all week. Then children visit a more affluent father on weekends, who buys them elaborate toys and clothing the mother cannot afford. One example was a father who stopped paying support to the children's mother, then entertained the children at a hotel on weekends, allowing them to run up large room-service charges.

The large number of stepfamilies in America has led to some complications in the laws of child support and child custody. Sometimes fathers, just like Cinderella's, will form another family and not take as much care of their children from their first marriage.

If you and your husband divorce, you may find your husband reluctant to agree about some items of support for your mutual children. Sometimes this is your husband's way of getting back at you. Other times it merely reflects something you knew for a long time while you were married—your husband likes to control spending. This can lead to scores of petty arguments with a former husband. You may assume an interpretation of support that may be different from your husband's. Don't assume anything. When Mary and her husband, Jim, divorced, the decree said her husband would take care of medical expenses.[9] Although he could have perfectly well afforded it, her husband refused to pay dental expenses. Mary had assumed that medical and dental were one and the same. She could not have imagined that her husband would be reluctant to pay for the braces necessary for their two daughters. However, her divorce decree did not specify.

Her husband was using his money to control a situation, the same thing he had done during Mary and Jim's marriage. If you expect your husband to help pay for your children's education, be sure you are specific: Do you mean college? Graduate school?

If you are divorced and your husband has not paid child support, trying to collect can be frustrating. You can hire a private attorney. But frequently women cannot afford to do that. You can go to various state agencies to try and collect. The state agencies that help women collect back child support are often tied to the welfare departments of the state, and many women are reluctant to go to such bureaus. One of the most effective ways of getting child support that is owed to you is to get a payroll deduction order: The money is taken from your husband's salary and he cannot stop it. But getting any results takes a lot of time and energy. A delinquent father can say he has paid. (Note the use of *father* here, instead of the currently popular usage *noncustodial parent;* 90 percent of the non-payers are the fathers.) Then the agencies have to weigh your word against his. Enforcement of payment of child support is also regulated by the courts, including the right to garnish wages to collect unpaid support. On October 25, 1992, Congress enacted the Child Support Recovery Act, making violation of support obligations by out-of-state fathers a felony. Credit agencies that request the information can report unpaid child support as debt, thus giving delinquent fathers bad credit ratings.

Fathers who do not pay child support are often supporting another family. Then they use the second family as an excuse for not paying the children of their first family. Not even Solomon would be able to solve some of the complicated financial problems of the modern American blended family. In New York State, if a father has one set of children from a first family, his first wife can get an order to deduct money from his salary, which takes priority over the needs of his second family—that is, unless he can show that the children of the second family will be worse off than the children from the first family.

Do You Want Your Children to Be Rich?

Child support, at least until the age of majority, is a "right" of American children, but inheritance is left to the largess of the parents.

In America, unlike France, it is not illegal for a man to disinherit his children, except in formerly French Louisiana. Reasons for disinheriting children can be complex. One Manhattan lawyer, Fred, originally from Oklahoma, moved to New York with his wife and two children. Then his wife left him for one of his best friends. Fred eventually met a lawyer who had children of her own. When Fred died of a heart attack after a vigorous tennis game, he was in his early forties. His two sons were in their teens. His will left all his money to his new girlfriend, trusting her to take care of his children.

If you decide you do not want to leave money to your children, you had better prepare a will saying so. Without a will the intestate laws of your state will provide for your children. This usually means children will inherit between one third and one half of your estate. Should your children inherit money when they are below the age of majority—between the ages of eighteen and twenty-one, depending on the state—that money would be put into a trust.

Chances are, unlike Cinderella's mother, you will outlive your husband, and therefore be able to provide for your children. But what if you die first? Here's where property ownership can become extremely important. If you and your husband live in a common law state the situation is as follows. If all of your property is in your husband's name, then you cannot designate how any of it should be dispersed should you die. If you and your husband own your property jointly, as many couples do, and it is as joint ownership with right of survivorship, it will go to your husband. *Tenants in common* means you own the property together, although not necessarily equally. But you can each leave your share to anyone you want at death. In other words, if you own your house as tenants in common, you could leave your half to your children, in trust if they are minors.

If you live in a community property state, you have rights to half the marital property, and can leave your half to your children. Your husband can do the same. Sometimes this can create problems, however. Be sure your husband hasn't put you in a position where you might be forced to sell your house before you want to because he gave his share to his children.

While you probably don't want to see your children left with nothing, it's important to balance your own needs with what you would like to leave to them. Americans are living for a very long time and spending much of their money on their own retirement and medical care. Many parents also spend a great deal of money on their children's education. Many also help their married children buy a house. So, often, there is not that much money left to leave to children. But as your assets increase, it's a good idea to talk with your husband about exactly what you would like to do for them.

If you each have children from a first marriage, you may again discover very different money attitudes that could cause problems. You may think children should have a regular allowance, no strings attached, while your husband may think an allowance is something that a child must earn. You may want to scrimp and save to send your children to an Ivy League college; your husband may think a state school like the one he attended is good enough. He may be of the "I did it myself" school and believe very little money should be left for the children. You may believe that children could greatly benefit from the security of some money that they knew would be theirs.

Money left for a child by a parent can also be interpreted by the child as a token of the parent's love. Not leaving money can send a message that a parent may not have intended.

Some months ago, my husband and I were talking to an English friend of ours who had twin boys. We were surprised to discover that our friend planned to leave more to the first-born twin. Unlike the French, who divide property equally among their children, the English adopted primogeniture—leaving all the property to the first-born son. When the English came to the New World they too adopted the system. Thomas Jefferson abolished primogeniture. Americans tend to want to leave equal amounts to each child. Of course, one does hear stories of parents who left unequal amounts of money thinking one child was well provided for. Not infrequently the well-off child suffers financial reverses when it is too late to change the will.

Should you decide to leave money for your children, you also have to decide how old they should be when they get the money. Lawyers have a tendency to suggest money be left in trust for a long time. A good solution is to leave the money so that it is gradually given to your children, say one half at age thirty and the balance at age forty. Leaving money outright to children could pose a problem should the children divorce. If you know that you will leave money to a son or daughter, you might discuss with your children the way in which they would like the money left. Remember, in some states there is no distinction between separate and marital property when couples divorce. You might suggest that they have pre-nuptial agreements so that they can keep their inherited money separate. And depending on how the money is used, separate money can quickly become marital. When leaving money for your children, there is also a question of trustees. You need to pick people who will outlive you and be able to manage that money for a long time. Naming one child as trustee for another child may not be the best solution.

Many men still think women are not capable of handling money. Most daughters still can't persuade their fathers to let them take over the family business. When there are family businesses, fathers frequently think of bringing in their sons, but only bring in daughters as a last resort.[10]

Despite the changes made in women's lives, fathers tend to see their daughters as producers of grandchildren. They leave wills that put money in trust for their daughters while leaving money outright to their sons.

If you are remarried and have children from your first marriage, remember that the law requires certain money to go to your current husband. If you have a pension, you must name your husband as a beneficiary and he must name you. That means that a husband of a short marriage will take precedence in receiving your pension benefits over your children from a first, long marriage.[11] The only way to avoid this is by having your husband sign a waiver of his survivor's rights to your pension money. You should discuss this before you marry. You also must check to be sure your particular pension plan will allow you to name someone other than your husband as a beneficiary.

Your husband is also entitled to a minimum share of your assets under the elective share laws of the state in which you live. If you want to leave all your money to your children, be sure you have a signed agreement from your husband—before you marry.

10.
What's It Worth?

When Samuel Newhouse, the publisher, died in 1979 the IRS claimed that his estate owed an additional $609 million in taxes, based on their appraisals of the value of Mr. Newhouse's minority interest in Advance Publications, Inc., and Newhouse Broadcasting, Inc. Eleven years later, U. S. Tax Court Judge B. John Williams, Jr., ruled against the IRS and settled for the $48 million the estate had originally submitted. The deciding factor was the judge's acceptance of the valuation placed on the stock as defined by the experts brought in by the Newhouse tax consultants.[1]

While the tax act of 1984 has eliminated any taxes on transfers of property between husband and wife, valuation of property still plays an important role in estate and divorce decisions.

Valuation becomes especially important if your husband is a partner in a small business. For example, if the partnership agreement states that the wife of a deceased partner is to be paid out in cash, how the partnership is valued can make an extraordinary difference in the amount of money you will receive.

When George Davidson died recently, he left shares of a privately owned company as part of his estate. Under the terms of his divorce agreement from a previous marriage, George had left one third of his estate rather than a specific dollar amount to his first wife. The remainder went to his second wife.

His first wife wanted to see a high value placed on the shares because, although they could not be sold publicly, she would be paid out in cash based on the value of the shares.

Still another group had an interest in the valuing of the shares. The stock brokerage firm that issued the stock wanted the value of the stocks to remain high. If not, the brokerage firm would have to devalue its net worth, a substantial portion of which is based on the stock. The company had been sold shortly before George's death. It went from being a company with substantial assets to being a company with a considerable debt. The husband had exchanged his shares for shares in the acquiring company.

An initial evaluation of the company made by the new owners valued the shares at $600,000. The brokerage firm revalued the shares at $400,000. When the executors hired an independent evaluation company, the stock was revalued as being worthless. In the meantime, the first wife had been paid her share of the stock, based on the second evaluation ($125,000).

If you and your husband divorce, his pension and yours could be your largest assets other than your home. Yet determining what it is worth for purposes of division in a divorce is not as simple as might be thought.

In many states, pensions are considered marital property whcn they are accumulated during the marriage. In a few states pensions are considered earnings and not marital property. Some states consider a pension as alimony, and other states regard it as a property award. If a pension is a property award, you would receive your share of it even if you remarried, but if a pension is considered alimony and you remarried, your payments would stop. Nevertheless, when it comes to evaluation many problems arise.

Even the date to use for determining the value of a pension plan, since the benefits are in the future, is a cause for conflict. Do you use:

The date of marital separation?
The date of filing of complaint?
The date of hearing or trial?

In Indiana, Richard N. Skirvin's pension vested thirty-two days after his divorce decree was entered. Even though his marriage lasted twenty-three years, his pension was not considered marital property and his wife received no part of it.[2]

Many other variables must be considered when trying to determine the value of a pension plan. For instance, what rate of interest should be used? What age will be used for the husband's retirement?

In a defined benefit plan, the pension amount is constantly accruing and has a value that is determinable at any time, including into the future. But, again, with future figures there can be variables such as fluctuating interest rates.

Frequently, when it comes to the division of pensions,

women lose out. In Massachusetts, for example, the husband is generally awarded his pension as part of the division of property: The usual practice is to value the benefits as of the date of divorce and treat them as a setoff for other assets that will be assigned to the wife. The result is that the wife often receives no retirement benefits from the marriage; instead she gets 50 percent of the present value.

You must also remember that if you are paid out for a pension plan that your husband will not collect for ten years, you are given a discounted value of the money. In other words, the value of a dollar that will be paid in ten years is less today. Experts use tables called discounted or present value tables to determine what that amount will be.

Here is an example of how a seemingly large pension award can vanish:

Amount of pension ten years out	Rate of interest	Amount you get
$100	5%	$61.39

In the past few years as more and more states have recognized the marital property value of pensions three basic methods of valuing pensions for divorce have evolved.

In the first method, the value of the pension is simply the amount of money that the employee has contributed, plus the accrued interest. The second method looks at the future benefits and then discounts those benefits to arrive at a present value. There are a number of variables in this method, including whether or not the employer will actually still be in business, and how long after retirement the employee will continue to live.

In a recent Maryland divorce, the husband's pension was valued at $122,936.87 because only his contributions to the plan and interest were considered. Had the second valuation method been used, the pension would have had a value of $358,034.22.[3] The wife was able to appeal the original valuation of her husband's pension. But for many women, the high cost of such an appeal would rule out any chance of doing so.

Another way that a woman can lose out when dividing pension benefits is on the assumption of a retirement date. The longer your husband works at his job, the more money he can accumulate in his pension. Yet many pension evaluations are made based on the earliest age at which your husband might retire, usually age sixty-two. This means the amount of money you might be awarded would be less than the amount your husband will actually receive.

Valuation of stocks that are listed on a stock exchange is simple. There is a definite price for a particular day.

Valuation of a stock option—an agreement to buy a stock at a specific price at a future date—is not as easy. Do the options have any value before they are exercised? That is one question that could arise in a divorce action. Naturally, experts for your husband would try and say that an unexercised option has no value. If this happens, ask your husband to give you all of his valueless options. The hope is that the price of the stock will rise. The option will allow you to buy the stock at a lower price and you will have a built-in profit.

Not having access to the company records puts one at

a great disadvantage. In a divorce it is generally the wife who therefore suffers. If a wife who did not work in a business is paid out by her late husband's partners, not having all the records could also be a disadvantage when it comes to valuing inventory.

Valuation of a privately held company or a professional practice differ in divorce or estate appraisals.

If your husband is the key person running the business and he suddenly dies, the value of the company may diminish considerably. But, if you divorce, the value of the company wouldn't change. Experts refer to this as the multiple—the number that would be used to establish the company's fair market value. There are several methods that can be used. Sometimes it is a multiple of earnings. If the man who ran the business dies, that number might drop to 2, whereas if he is still alive and running the company, in a divorce action, the multiple might be 6. In other words, the business would be worth more or less depending on the key person. Of course, in a divorce action your husband's lawyers would say, "Mr. Jones is very valuable. If something happened to him there would be no business." Your husband's lawyers would want to use a low multiple. Your lawyer would claim that "the business could be run by a monkey." He would try and establish a high multiple by suggesting "There's no cult of personality."

Some businesses have what are called buy-sell agreements. One partner agrees to buy out the other at a specific price. Often these agreements are written with the tax collector in mind, and so have values that are considerably lower than the actual worth of the business. If you own a business and the partners have agreed to pay your estate should you die, you must be sure you have an up-to-date buy-sell agreement that truly reflects the value of the business—otherwise your heirs could lose out. If your husband has a business, be sure he has taken a recent look at the buy-sell agreement. It may have to be revalued.

Medical and legal practices are assets that must frequently be valued in a divorce settlement, unless you and your husband have agreed in a prenuptial agreement that you will keep your practices out of any divorce negotiations. If a medical or legal practice is part of a divorce agreement, be sure you have an appraiser who specializes in evaluating medical practices, not just a general appraiser. When a medical practice is evaluated for a divorce, "goodwill" is often disputed. Goodwill is the value imputed to the business, above and beyond the actual assets. In other words, if your husband is a doctor, how much are his actual reputation, client list, and special skills worth, above the actual medical equipment, accounts receivable, value of the office lease, etc.? Obviously, medical and legal practices are worth more when your husband is alive and able to practice than if your husband dies and you try to sell his practice to another doctor. In a divorce, the goodwill would have some value, but without your husband, the practice would be worth much less; there would be no goodwill.

Valuing works of art can also be extremely difficult. For one thing you have to value a work that is unique.[4] Different definitions can apply. If a work of art is given as a charitable contribution, the IRS will look to a comparable work of art. For estate taxes, the criterion is for a fair market value. For insurance purposes, you might want to know the replacement value. This is not the value you would use for estate tax purposes or equitable distribution in a divorce case.

Questions to ask an appraiser:

1. Have you dealt specifically with this field before? You would not want a jewelry appraiser to value your African sculpture.
2. How will you substantiate the price—e.g., auction catalogues, other dealers?
3. How will you charge? Be careful of the art appraiser who is charging a percentage of the appraised value. According to Victor Wiener of the Appraisers Association of America, the IRS will not accept an appraisal that is based on a percentage of the appraised value unless it's for estate or gift taxes.[5]

The more information you have about the work, the better. For example, if you know that a work was published, and you can provide its provenance, you may be able to show that the work has a greater value. Remember, too, that just because a dealer asks a high price for a work of art, does not mean that the work will be sold at that price. The same technique would apply to all types of appraisal.

11.
1040

Q. And you saw the tax returns on an annual basis. Is that right?

A. Yes.

Q. I take it you reviewed the returns before you signed them, didn't you?

A. Frankly, I didn't. I trusted [my husband] completely.

Q. Weren't you curious, whether you trusted him or not, as to the state of the family finances?

A. Frankly, no.

Q. Did you ever keep copies of the returns which you signed?

A. I didn't have them.

The speaker in the above dialogue is a female executive with an annual salary of over $300,000. This is a transcript from her divorce proceedings. When it came to finances, like many women she reverted to the traditional role of the wife. No matter that in her own job she oversaw huge budgets and made financial commitments affecting hundreds of employees. At home her husband managed the finances, hired the accountants, and she signed on the appropriate lines.

The tax return is frequently the husband's job, just as mowing the lawn is considered his domain. Husbands don't necessarily do the taxes because they want to keep things from their wives. They do the taxes because their wives don't want to touch them.

As a result, the tax return has become a mystery to many women and therefore a great weapon when it comes time for a divorce. Smart lawyers pore over the tax return looking for hidden assets and income. The discovery of an outstanding loan might signify the existence of a net worth statement that could be used to demand more in divorce settlements. Many women don't even have copies of a tax return for which they are jointly liable should there be a problem with underpayment.

By the way, if you do not have copies of your tax returns, you can get them from the IRS. To request a copy of a return you need Form 4506 available by calling a local office. The problem is, getting the returns could take months, which you don't want to waste if you are getting a divorce, and the government might only go back three or four years; your lawyer, on the other hand, might need more.

These days, you just might be the family member who prepares the tax returns, or you might do them with your husband. If you are not interested in the tax returns, you should be: It's part of the marriage.

The tax return can give you a good insight into your husband's attitude about money. Does he try to take business deductions for personal expenses? Is this how you would handle it? If it's not, knowing early on in your marriage could be helpful.

. . .

Here are three reasons you should read your tax return:

1. You might discover that your husband has less income than you thought.
2. You might discover that your husband has more income than you thought.
3. You might discover that your husband is cheating the government and because you are signing the returns you could be in trouble.

What the Tax Return Can Reveal: A Short Course in Reading Tax Returns [1]

The basic form 1040 is the clue to what's going on. It tells about taxable income and related investments. What follows is based on the 1040 as it appeared in 1993.

Income: This section of the tax return is on the first page. It lists different forms of income. Most are straightforward:

- wages, salaries, and tips
- taxable interest income (There is also a line for tax-exempt interest income that has been added to the return recently, but isn't always reported accurately.)
- dividend income
- capital gains (capital losses also would be listed here)— If your husband dabbled in the market and dropped a bundle, here's where it will appear.
- partnership income (This is of particular interest to

your divorce lawyer but it's also good to know about if
your husband dies or is disabled.)
• pensions and annuities
• business income or loss
• income from estates and trusts

What you won't find on the 1040 are some tax-free
investments. You would need the state income tax return
to find this. You also will not find investments that do not
pay interest. Foreign investment income, although it is
supposed to be listed on the 1040 and then filed as a
separate Form 90–22.1, may not be filed by everyone.
The existence of a life insurance policy does not show up
on a tax return either.

Adjustments to Income: This is the second most interesting section of the tax return. Here you may find an
IRA or a Keogh plan that your husband hadn't mentioned. You might even find alimony payments for a wife
you hadn't known about (including her Social Security
number). You should also check your husband's W-2
form to see if the box for any retirement plans is checked.

If you find a sudden increase in your husband's dona-
tion to a Keogh, it could mean he wants to reduce the
amount of his income—a possible sign that he could be
planning to leave the marriage.

You will not find any deferred compensation or deferred bonuses on a tax return.

Form 2106, Employee Business Expenses, is also an
interesting part of the tax return. Some of these expenses
may contribute to your family's standard of living. They
could include food, entertainment, telephone, and auto
expenses. It's important to understand what part of your

living expenses come from your husband's job and yours, if you both work, because in the event of a divorce your lawyer will want to figure this into the settlement.

Schedule D. Capital Gains and Losses: There's a lot to look at here. You are supposed to report the gain and loss you have from the sale of stocks, bonds, real estate, partnerships, the sale of your home, and income from trusts. What you are looking at is a number that does not always tell you about the underlying asset.

If, for example, you see that stock has been sold for $8,000 and there is a $2,000 loss, you want to be sure you know what happened to the proceeds of that sale. The return will just tell you about the loss, but not what happened to the $8,000.

You might see that there is partnership income but you will not be able to tell the value of the underlying property.

There might be income of $4,000 from a trust, but the trust could be worth $100,000 and your husband could control the assets.

If you see interest income from bonds, you can sometimes work backward to get an approximate idea of their underlying value. If you see $3,600 in income and you use a rate of interest of 6 percent, you would know that there had to be an asset worth around $60,000.

If you and your husband both work and you are planning to take time off to have a family, looking at reimbursed expenses, in addition to your salary, will give you a better idea of how much different your way of life might be on only one income.

If you and your husband divorce and you are asking for support, the amount of support is often based on the standard of living. If your lawyer can show that you and your husband had a way of life that was based partly on his salary and partly on expenses that were reimbursed by his employer, you might receive more support.

If you and your husband are divorcing, you should also look at some of the deductions that might artificially reduce income. These would include noncash charitable contributions or any type of casualty or theft loss. This could be important for alimony.

If you and your husband are planning to retire and you want to consider how much money you will spend, just looking at your salaries might lead you to underestimate the amount of money you would both need. Adding in your reimbursed expenses to your salaries would give you a more realistic amount.

If you and your husband are also taking a look at how you might manage as a widow, you would also want to consider these expenses.

How Taxes Work If You Are Divorced

You can transfer tax-free money between husband and wife. What you can't do is pass off alimony, which would require tax payments, as marital exchange. Alimony is usually tax deductible by the payor and taxable to the recipient. If you, the wife, receive alimony, you must pay taxes on it. If you, the wife, pay alimony to your former husband, you deduct it and he pays the taxes.

So as not to disguise cash transfer (not tax-deductible by the payee) as alimony (deductible by the payor), the laws are quite specific about what counts as alimony. For example, if you receive a lump-sum payment of $100,000 and it is given in three years, you can be paid in equal installments for three years or you can be paid in decreasing amounts, providing it is not more than $15,000 each year. Thus many alimony settlements are really property settlements in disguise. Alimony must stop when the payor dies, and can only be paid when husband and wife are living separately.

If one spouse has a very low income and the other a very high income, you can negotiate which of you gets the deduction. Sometimes this is a point of negotiations in a divorce proceeding.

If you keep the marital home as part of your divorce settlement and you then sell it, you will have to pay the taxes if there are any capital gains. The cost of the house will be considered the price you paid when you and your husband bought the house, not the price the house may have been when you and your husband divorced. Courts often do not figure the capital gains taxes when dividing property. So what seems like an equal split can cost you money. Remember that you do have two options that could blunt the blow: You could roll over the profits into another house within two years and not pay taxes on the appreciation, or you could, if you are over fifty-five, take advantage of the $125,000 exclusion.

If you get a cash payment of part of your husband's pension before his retirement age, that money must be rolled over into an IRA—within sixty days, or you will have to pay taxes on it. If you are getting this pension money and need to use it right away, you will be getting less money than you thought. A cash settlement of $100,000 and a pension settlement of $100,000 have different tax implications. The $100,000 in cash is a transfer, no taxes due. The $100,000 in pension money has income tax consequences when you eventually take the money out. You would have to pay a 10 percent penalty for using the money before he is fifty-nine and a half. You would also have to pay any income tax that was due.

Property settlements are not taxable because they are treated as a transfer between husband and wife. But if there is appreciated value, the tax would have to be paid when the property is sold. For example, if you transfer stock from husband to wife that cost $60,000 and is now worth $100,000, the wife would have to pay the taxes on the $40,000. This has to be figured into the settlement.

Child support is not tax deductible. The government does allow you to deduct children as dependents. Sometimes the deduction is negotiated as part of the settlement.

Retirement Taxes[2]

Money that is stashed away in a tax-deferred account—such as an IRA or a Keogh plan—becomes taxable income when it is withdrawn upon your retirement. If you withdraw the money before you retire, you not only pay the income taxes but you pay a penalty for taking the money out before you should. (In 1993 the magic number is fifty-nine and a half years.) The theory here is that you will be in a lower tax bracket when you retire than when you are working so the taxes won't be so bad.

If you change jobs, are fired, or have a retirement plan

that is ending, you could also receive a lump-sum payout. As mentioned, this money has to be reinvested in another plan or a roll-over IRA in order for you to avoid paying income taxes and a penalty. If you receive your money in a lump-sum payout and are over fifty-nine and a half you can take advantage of forward averaging tax breaks.

If your husband had an IRA and you are the beneficiary, you will receive a lump-sum payment. If this is rolled over into another IRA you will not have to pay taxes. When you retire you can receive all of your IRA funds in a lump sum.

Starting in 1994 you will have to pay taxes on 85 percent of your Social Security benefits if your overall joint income is $44,000 or if you are single with an income of $34,000 or higher. Fifty percent of your benefits are taxed if you are single and your income is over $25,000 or you have a joint income over $32,000.

If you are over fifty-five and you sell your house, you do not have to pay capital gains on up to $125,000 of profit. Remember, however, this is a one-shot, one-house-per-couple deal. If you are married to someone who has taken his onetime write-off, you and he as a couple cannot claim this benefit again. If you know you are going to remarry and have not taken your benefit but your husband-to-be has already used his, sell your house before you remarry. You must have lived in the house for three years. Remember, too, that if you had previously deferred profits on a house sale, by buying another house your tax base would be reduced by that amount. Here's an example of how this works:

House A was purchased for: $ 50,000
House A was sold for: $100,000
House B was purchased for: $150,000 (tax basis for House
B is $100,000)
House B was sold for: $350,000 (gain would be
$250,000)
The exclusion would be: $125,000
Taxes would be due on: $125,000

If you and your husband are eligible to receive your retirement money in a lump sum, known as lump sum distribution, you can put it into a roll-over IRA within sixty days of the payout, and keep that money tax deferred. You would pay income taxes on the amounts you withdraw, but presumably at a rate lower than you paid when you were working.

ESTATE AND INHERITANCE TAXES

No estate taxes are owed to the federal government on any amount a husband leaves to a wife or a wife to a husband. State governments have different rules; in some states you may have taxes to pay.

Each of us is entitled to a lifetime exemption of $600,000 to leave money without incurring any federal estate taxes. This is known as the unified gift and estate tax. If you have $700,000 and leave it to your husband, he pays no taxes when you die. When he dies, he can leave $600,000 tax free, but estate taxes will be due on the other $100,000. Not all states conform to the federal lifetime exemption.

Estate taxes owed to the federal government must be

paid nine months after the date of death, except for closely held businesses or in cases where hardship can be shown. If you have commercial real estate that has suffered a substantial drop in value the government might not force you to sell at a loss in order to pay taxes. You might be able to make a deal to defer payment.

If you inherit the family house from your husband, you own the house at the amount it is worth when your husband died, not at the price your husband paid for it. This is known as getting a step-up basis in value. Therefore, you do not pay any taxes on the appreciation between the time your husband bought the house and you inherited it.

Tax laws are constantly changing and difficult to understand. A good accountant is probably the best person to ask about taxes. If you don't have one, ask friends for suggestions, make appointments, interview a few, and then make your choice.

Afterword

In the 1970s Barbara Walters could speculate about whether she would have to marry for money. But in the 1990s Joan Lunden can tell her the answer. A Westchester County court recently ordered Joan Lunden, TV anchorwoman, to pay her husband of fourteen years $18,000 a month in temporary support. Miss Lunden wondered why her husband couldn't just go out and get a job.

The nineties could be the decade when women finally come into their own. And while this doesn't mean the end of the wife who stays home to take care of her family, it should mean the end of the wife who doesn't know what is going on. Taking financial responsibility is part of the process. It would be naïve to suggest that the laws work perfectly, but at least they exist. The direction is right. The laws are in place to allow us an equal stake in the workplace. Women also have equal property rights. Now, the battle that was waged by so many women to secure these rights must be waged by individual women in their homes.

Marriage is here to stay. And while our legal system continues to define the property rights for death and divorce, we must make our own rules for our marriages. We must reeducate our husbands and sons to see a different role for women. But, equally important, we must educate our daughters to their responsibilities as well.

I believe that knowledge of family finances will help. Women have to participate in financial decisions. And women have to take responsibility for their own financial futures. Every woman should know about her pension, her will, her health insurance as well as her husband's. Every woman should recognize that even in the best of marriages, her financial interests may differ from her husband's. You should know how the decisions you and your husband make will affect your future. If you have children from a previous marriage and assets you want to leave them, you should know how the laws of your state about marriage, divorce, and death can affect your ownership of property.

It doesn't mean that you have to be able to invest money like a pro, but it does mean you should know when you need a pro, who the pros are, and how to choose them. If your husband is good at it, let him do it. But if he's not, you must not be afraid to ask questions and to participate in the process of his decisions.

It doesn't even mean that you have to earn big bucks, but you should know about the money you and your husband have accumulated.

Women have spent their years taking care of their homes, their husbands, their children, and, increasingly, their parents. It's time women started taking care of their finances. It doesn't mean that you are planning a divorce;

it merely means that you are realistic about the possibility and prepared should it happen.

The key is knowledge and participation, instead of control and abdication.

Remember, it's your money too. Think of it that way.

Notes

1. MARRIAGE IS NOT AN EQUAL OPPORTUNITY

1. Kagan, Julia, and Rosalind C. Barnett, "Money Mastery," *Working Woman* (December 1986), p. 71.
2. In 1960, 230 women and 9,010 men were awarded law degrees. In 1989, women received 14,519 law degrees, men 21,048. In 1960 women received 387 medical degrees from American schools; men received 6,645. In 1989, women received 5,128 medical degrees, men received 10,326.
3. Voydanoff, Patricia, "Economic Distress and Family Relations: A Review of the Eighties," *Journal of Marriage and the Family* (November 1990), p. 1100.
4. Potuchek, Jean L., "Who's Responsible for Supporting the Family? Employed Wives and the Breadwinner Role," Wellesley College, Center for Research on Women (1988), p. 3.
5. Interview, Susan Hayward, senior vice president, Yankelovitch, Monitor (August 7, 1992).
6. U.S. Bureau of Census Population Reports P-20 No. 458, *Household and Family Characteristics.* Washington, D.C.: U.S. Government Printing Office, 1991, p. 247.
7. Current Population Survey, March 1993, income supplement. Bureau of the Census, Consumer Income Report Series, P60–184.

8. Shelton, Beth Ann, "The Distribution of Household Tasks, Does Wife's Employment Make a Difference," *Journal of Family Issues* (June 1990), pp. 131–32.

9. Blumberg, Rae Lesser, and Marion Tolbert Coleman, "A Theoretical Look at the Gender Balance of Power in the American Couple," *Journal of Family Issues* (June 1990), p. 241.

10. Jeanhee Kim, "Where Women Stand," *Working Woman* (January 1994), p. 31.

11. Bernstein, Daniel, "For In-House Women, the Story Differs," *National Law Journal* (1992).

12. Crouter, Ann, in Menghan and Parcel, p. 1090; and Stanley, Sandra C., Janet G. Hunt, and Larry L. Hunt, "The Relative Deprivation of Husbands in Dual-Earner Households," *Journal of Family Issues* (March 1986), pp. 3–20.

13. Lewin, Tamar, "For Some Two-Paycheck Families, the Economics Don't Add Up," *New York Times* (April 21, 1991) p. 18; Johnson, Elizabeth Richie, "I Couldn't Afford My Job," *Redbook* (April 21, 1991), p. 89; and Potuchek, p. 7.

14. White, Lynn K., and Shengming Tang, "The Economic Foundations of Marital Happiness and Divorce," paper presented at Midwest Sociological Society, St. Louis, Mo. (April 1991), unpublished.

15. White and Tang, ibid.

16. Survey, Oppenheimer Management Corporation (March 1992), unpublished.

17. Bumpass, Larry, James Sweet, and Teresa Castro, "Changing Patterns of Remarriage." University of Wisconsin (August 1988), unpublished paper, p. 4.

18. Schoen, Robert, et al., "Marriage and Divorce in Twentieth Century American Cohorts," *Demography* (February 1985) p. 101.

19. Norton, Arthur J., and Louisa F. Miller, *Marriage, Divorce and Remarriage in the 1990s,* Current Population Reports P23–180, Bureau of the Census, Washington, D.C., U.S. Government Printing Office, 1992, p. 5.

20. Ibid., p. 5.

21. Dobris, Joel C., "Medicaid Asset Planning by the Elderly: A Policy View of Expectations, Entitlement and Inheritance," *Real Property, Probate and Trust Journal* (Spring 1989), p. 3.

2. I Do, I Do

1. Wortman, Marlene Stein, ed. *Women in American Law,* Vol. 1, *From Colonial Times to the New Deal.* New York: Holmes and Meier, 1985, p. 112.
2. Wortman, p. 372. An excellent article to read about women's rights is by Mary Moers Wenig, "The Marital Property Law of Connecticut: Past, Present and Future," *Wisconsin Law Review* (1990), pp. 807–879.
3. Weisbert, Lynn, "A Marriage Made . . . by Satellite?" *National Law Journal* (March 4, 1991), p. 39.
4. *Pappas* v. *Pappas,* 300 S. C. 62, 386 S. E. 2d 468, South Carolina Court Appeal, 1989.
5. *Ullah* v. *Ullah* Decisions, Second Judicial Department Kings County, 1A Part 5, Justice Rigler, November 8, 1988.

3. Marriage, Inc.

1. Schultz, Ellen, "When It's the Wrong Time for Big Financial Decisions," *The Wall Street Journal* (October 29, 1991), p. C3.
2. Consumer Expenditures for 1992, Bureau of Labor Statistics.
3. "Study: Her 2nd trip down the aisle likely to be his first," *New York Post* (August 26, 1991), p. 15.
4. Helene Brezinsky, New York, shared her list of mistakes with me. This list incorporates some of her material.

4. "Honey, Just Sign Here"

1. *Neilson* v. *Neilson,* 780 P. 2d 1264 (Utah, 1989); Freed, Doris Jonas, and Timothy B. Walker, eds., "Family Law in the Fifty States: An Overview," *Family Law Quarterly* (Winter 1991), p. 392.
2. *Baylor Law Review* (1990), p. 830; *Wade* v. *Austin,* 5243 Wnd at 86.
3. *D'Amato* v. *D'Amato,* 176 So. 2d 907.
4. *Lutgert* v. *Lutgert,* 338 So. 2d 1111 October 27, 1976.

5. "Chronicle," *New York Times* (January 1, 1991), p. 59.
6. *McKee-Johnson* v. *Johnson,* 444 N.W. 2d 259 (Minnesota 1989), in Freed and Walker, p. 391.
7. *Mixon* v. *Mixon,* 550 So. 2d 999 (Alabama Civil Appeals, 1989), in Freed and Walker, p. 393.
8. *Gross* v. *Gross,* 464 NE Reporter Second Series, 11 Ohio St 3d 99 No 83-564, Supreme Court of Ohio, June 13, 1984, p. 500.

5. COMING APART

1. Riley, Glenda. *Divorce: An American Tradition.* New York: Oxford University Press, 1991, pp. 12–16, 133.
2. Sheppard, Annamay, T., "Women, Families and Equality: Was Divorce Reform a Mistake?" *Women's Rights Law Reporter* (Fall 1990), p. 144.
3. *New Jersey Shore Medical Center–Fitkin Hospital* v. *Baum's Estate,* 84 N. J. 137, 417 A. 2d 1003 (1980), in Sheppard, p. 145.
4. While these states do not have specific statutes that recognize the so-called "housewife's" contribution, the courts may still consider the contribution when dividing marital assets; Timothy Walker, editor, "Family Law in the Fifty States," *Family Law Quarterly,* (Winter 1990), p. 539.
5. *Ford* v. *Ford,* 766 p. 2d 950.
6. Interview with Peter Roth, lawyer for Mrs. Goldman, July 28, 1991; *Goldman* v. *Goldman,* "Findings of Fact and Conclusions of Law," Department of the Trial Court, Probate and Family Court, Docket No. 86D-0125-D1 (May 10, 1988).
7. Brown, Ronald L. "Case Developments," *Fairshare* (January 1990), p. 25.
8. Abraham, Jed H., "*The Divorce Revolution* Revisited: A Counterrevolutionary Critique," *American Journal of Family Law* (Summer 1989), p. 103.
9. Singer, Jana B., "Divorce Reform and Gender Justice," *The North Carolina Law Review* (June 1989), pp. 1103–5.

6. If You Thought Marriage Was Bad . . .

1. Wardle, Lynn D., "No-Fault Divorce and the Divorce Conundrum," *Brigham Young University Law Review* (1991), pp. 79–142; Sheppard, Annamay T., "Women, Families and Equality: Was Divorce Reform a Mistake?" *Women's Rights Law Reporter* (Fall 1990), pp. 143–152.
2. Interviews with Peter Roth, September 27, 1990.
3. Report of the Gender Bias Study of the Supreme Judicial Court, Commonwealth of Massachusetts, 1989. The Massachusetts gender bias study revealed that "Eighty-five percent of the lawyers responding to the family law survey said that courts rarely or never award adequate counsel fees in advance. Sixty-eight percent reported that judges rarely or never award adequate expert witness fees."
4. Schafran, Lynn Hecht, "Gender Bias in the Courts: An Emerging Focus for Judicial Reform," *Arizona State Law Journal* (1989), p. 239.
5. Anderson, Cerisse, "Football Player's Retirement Held a Waste of Marital Asset," *New York Law Journal* (July 1989), p. 1.
6. Belin, David W. *Leaving Money Wisely: Creative Estate Planning for Middle and Upper-Income Americans for the 1990s.* New York: Charles Scribner's Sons, 1990, p. 98.
7. Sherman, Rorie, "Billed for Sex?" *National Law Journal* (August 1991).
8. *Smith* v. *Smith*, 90 Daily Journal DAR 13732, *Matrimonial Strategist* (January 1991), p. 2.

7. Retirement? For Whom?

1. Aries, Philippe, and Georges Duby, eds. *A History of Private Life from Pagan Rome to Byzantium,* Vol. I. Cambridge, Mass.: The Belknap Press of Harvard University Press, 1987, p. 459.
2. Unpublished statistics. Frederick W. Hollmann, "U.S. Population Estimates by Age, Sex, Race, and Hispanic Origin 1990–1992," Bureau of the Census.
3. Dobris, Joel C., "Medicaid Asset Planning by the Elderly: A Policy View of Expectations, Entitlement and Inheritance," *Real Property, Probate and Trust Journal* (Spring 1989), p. 7.

4. Stern, Fritz. *Gold and Iron.* New York: Alfred A. Knopf, 1977, pp. 208–209.

5. Bernstein, Aaron, "In Search of the Vanishing Nest Egg," *Business Week,* July 30, 1990, p. 46.

6. Congress established Individual Retirement Accounts in 1986. At that time, you could deduct from your income, thus lowering your tax bracket, the amount of money you put into your IRA. The money could then be invested tax free. Recently, however, the rules for IRAs changed. If your income is above $25,000 or your joint income is above $40,000, tax deductions for an IRA are phased out if you or your husband are covered by another plan. If a wife wants to open her own pension fund account because she works for a company that does not provide a pension plan, she would have to count her husband's income as well as her own in establishing eligibility to deduct her contribution from her salary.

7. Bureau of the Census, Statistical Abstract of the United States, 1992. Washington, D.C.: U.S. Government Printing Office (1993), p. 363.

8. "Heading for Hardship: Retirement Income for American Women in the Next Century," *Older Women's League* (May 1990), p. 8.

9. Bernstein, *Business Week* (July 30, 1990).

10. Rosefsky, Bob. *Money Talks.* New York: McGraw-Hill Publishing Company, 1989, p. 535.

11. Health Insurance Association of America. *The Consumers Guide to Disability Insurance,* p. 1. [Statistics from Guardian Life, as quoted in "Disability Insurance," *Changing Times* (August 1990), p. 56.]

12. *Changing Times* (August 1990), p. 53.

13. "The Unaffordability of Nursing Home Insurance," A Families USA Foundation Report (January 1990), p. 4; *Consumers Guide to Long-term Care Insurance.* Washington, D.C.: Health Insurance Association of America (April 1989).

14. "The Unaffordability of Nursing Home Insurance," p. 2.

8. WILL POWER

1. Aries, Philippe, and Georges Duby, eds. *A History of Private Life from Pagan Rome to Byzantium,* Vol. I. Cambridge, Mass.: The Belknap Press of Harvard University Press, 1987, p. 31.

2. Collins, Herbert R., and David B. Weaver. *Wills of the Presidents of the United States.* New York: Communication Channels, Inc., 1976, pp. 19–28.
3. Roth, Nathan, M.D. *The Psychiatry of Writing a Will.* Springfield, Ill.: Charles C. Thomas, 1989, pp. 52–53.
4. Huffington, Arianna Stassinopoulos. *Picasso, Creator and Destroyer.* New York: Simon and Schuster, 1988, pp. 471–72.
5. Luncheon honoring Mrs. Vincent Astor, sponsored by the World Monuments Association, October 22, 1991.
6. "Family Fortunes," *Forbes* (October 17, 1994), p. 290.
7. Rosefsky, Bob. *Money Talks.* New York: McGraw-Hill, 1989, p. 568.
8. Tillman, Fred, and Susan G. Parker. *Your Will and Estate Planning.* Boston: Houghton Mifflin, 1990, p. 49.
9. Based on proposals from the New York Public Library.

9. CINDERELLA REVISED

1. Aries, Philippe, and Georges Duby, eds. *A History of Private Life from Pagan Rome to Byzantium,* Vol. I. Cambridge, Mass.: The Belknap Press of Harvard University Press, 1987, pp. 9–11.
2. Czapanskiy, Karen, "Volunteers and Draftees: The Struggle for Parental Equality," *UCLA Law Review* (1991), pp. 1415ff.
3. Buser, Paul J. "Introduction: The First Generation of Stepchildren," *Family Law Quarterly* (Spring 1991), p. 6.
4. Munsterman, Janice T., Claire B. Grimm, and Thomas A. Henderson, "A Summary of Child Support Guidelines," National Center for State Courts (February 1, 1990), p. 3.
5. Dodson, Diane, "A Guide to the Guidelines," *Family Advocate* (Spring 1988), p. 8.
6. Brett, Leslie J., Sharon Toffey Shepela, and Janet Kniffin, eds. "Women and Children Beware: The Economic Consequences of Divorce in Connecticut," Hartford College for Women, Women's Research Institute, Hartford, Conn. (1990), pp. 32–33.
7. Waldman, Steven, "Deadbeat Dads," *Newsweek* (May 4, 1992), p. 46.
8. Lester, Gordon H., "Child Support and Alimony: 1989," *Current Population Reports,* Consumer Income Series P-60, No. 173, Washington, D.C.: U.S. Government Printing Office, 1991, p. 1.

9. In 1990, only 40 percent of mothers receiving child support were also awarded health insurance benefits. Of these only two thirds complied. Lester, pp. 8–10.
10. Interview with John Messervey, family business consultant, Lake Forest, Illinois, 1982.
11. Wenig, Mary, "The Marital Property Law of Connecticut," *Wisconsin Law Review* (1990), pp. 807–79.

10. What's It Worth?

1. Garniau, George, "Newhouse Wins Tax Case," *Editor and Publisher* (March 10, 1990), pp. 12, 31.
2. *Skirvin* v. *Skirvin*, 560 NE2d 1263 (Indiana Appeals 1 District 1990).
3. *Imagnu* v. *Wodajo*, 582 Atlantic reporter, 2d Series, December 4, 1990. 85 Md. App. 208.
4. Lerner, Ralph E., "Putting a Price on Art," *The National Law Journal* (June 17, 1991).
5. Wiener, Victor, "Recent Cases Highlight Complications Involved in Selecting an Appraiser," *The National Law Journal* (June 17, 1991), p. S7.

11. 1040

1. Podell, Peggy, and M. Dee Samuels, eds. *The 1040 Handbook: A Guide to Income and Asset Discovery.* Chicago: American Bar Association, 1990.
2. An excellent guide to the retirement tax maze is *Maximizing Your Retirement Plan Distribution,* available at this writing from Charles Schwab, 101 Montgomery Street, San Francisco, Cal. 94104.

Bibliography

Books

Appel, Jens C. III, and F. Bruce Gentry. *The Complete Will Kit.* New York: John Wiley and Sons, 1990.

Aries, Philippe, and Georges Duby, eds. *A History of Private Life from Pagan Rome to Byzantium,* Vol. I. Cambridge, Mass.: The Belknap Press of Harvard University Press, 1987.

Belin, David W. *Leaving Money Wisely: Creative Estate Planning for Middle- and Upper-Income Americans for the 1990s.* New York: Charles Scribner's Sons, 1990.

Collins, Herbert R., and David B. Weaver. *Wills of the Presidents of the United States.* New York: Communication Channels, Inc., 1976.

Huffington, Arianna Stassinopoulos. *Picasso, Creator and Destroyer.* New York: Simon and Schuster, 1988.

Lewis, Naphtali, and Meyer Reinhold, eds. *Roman Civilization.* Vol. 1, *Selected Readings, the Republic and the Augustan Age.* New York: Columbia University Press, 1990.

McConaughey, Dan E. *Georgia: Divorce, Alimony, and Child Custody.* Norcross, Ga.: The Harrison Company, 1990.

Podell, Peggy, and M. Dee Samuels, eds. *The 1040 Handbook: A Guide to Income and Asset Discovery.* Chicago, Ill.: American Bar Association, 1990.

Raggio, Grier, Jr., Lowell K. Halverson, and John W. Kydd. *Divorce in New York: How to Negotiate Your Divorce Without Tears or Trial.* New York: Rutledge Books, 1987.

Riley, Glenda D. *Divorce: An American Tradition.* New York: Oxford University Press, 1991.

Rosefsky, Bob. *Money Talks.* New York: McGraw-Hill, 1989.

Roth, Nathan, M.D. *The Psychiatry of Writing a Will.* Springfield, Ill.: Charles C. Thomas, 1989.

Roth, T. *Babylonian Marriage Agreements, Seventh–Third Centuries, B.C.* Germany: Verlag, Butzon and Becker Kevelaer, 1989.

Shaw, George Bernard. *Collected Plays with Their Prefaces: Definitive Edition.* New York: Dodd, Mead & Company, 1971.

Stern, Fritz. *Gold and Iron.* New York: Alfred A. Knopf, 1977.

Weitzman, Lenore J. *The Marriage Contract: A Guide to Living with Lovers and Spouses.* New York: The Free Press, 1981.

Wortman, Marlene Stein, ed. *Women in American Law.* Vol. 1, *From Colonial Times to the New Deal.* New York: Holmes and Meier Publishers, 1985.

The World Almanac. New York: World Almanac Publications, 1992.

GOVERNMENT REPORTS

Bureau of the Census. Current Population Report. *Child Support and Alimony, 1989.* Consumer Income Series P60–173. 1989.

Bureau of the Census. Current Population Report. *Child Support and Alimony.* Consumer Income Series P23–154. 1985.

Department of Health and Human Services, Social Security Administration. *Retirement.* SSA Publication No. 05-10035. January 1991.

Department of Labor, Pension and Welfare Benefits Administration. *What You Should Know About the Pension Law: A Guide to the Employees Retirement Income Security Act of 1974, as Amended by the Retirement Equity Act of 1984, and the Tax Reform Act of 1986.* May 1988.

Supreme Judical Court, Commonwealth of Massachusetts. *Gender Bias Study of the Court System in Massachusetts.* 1989.

Reports

Brett, Leslie, Sharon Toffey Shepela, and Janet Kniffin. *Women and Children Beware: The Economic Consequences of Divorce in Connecticut.* Women's Research Institute, Hartford College for Women. Summer, 1990.

Erickson, Nancy S., *1993 Update, Child Support Manual for Legal Services.* National Center on Women and Family Law, Inc. New York, 1993.

Families USA Foundation. *The Unaffordability of Nursing Home Insurance.* Washington, D.C. January 1990.

Health Insurance Association of America. *Consumers Guide to Long-term Care Insurance.* Washington, D.C. April 1989.

———. *Consumers Guide to Disability Insurance.* Washington, D.C. July 1989.

McLanahan, Sara S., and Renee A. Monson. "Caring for the Elderly: Prevalence and Consequences," unpublished, 1989.

Munsterman, Janice T., Claire B. Grimm, and Thomas A. Henderson, *A Summary of Child Support Guidelines.* National Center for State Courts. February 1, 1990.

Older Women's League. *Heading for Hardship: Retirement Income for American Women in the Next Century.* Washington, D.C. May 1990.

Articles

Staff of *American Demographics* magazine. "The Rich Are Different from One Another." *Wall Street Journal* (November 12, 1990).

Barron, James. "In *Trump* v. *Trump*, the Focus Is on Lots of Fine Print." *The New York Times* (February 15, 1990).

Bernstein, Aaron. "In Search of the Vanishing Nest Egg: For Young Workers, Pensions May Be Going the Way of the Dodo." *Business Week* (July 30, 1990).

Bernstein, Daniel. "For In-House Women, the Story Differs." *National Law Journal* (1992).

Blumberg, Rae Lesser, and Marion Tolbert Coleman. "A Theoretical Look at the Gender Balance of Power in the American Couple." *Journal of Family Issues* (June 1990).

Brown, Ronald L., ed. "Partially Rehabilitated Spouse." *Fairshare: The Matrimonial Law Monthly* (January 1990).

Buser, Paul J. "Introduction: The First Generation of Stepchildren." *Family Law Quarterly* (Spring 1991).

Collins, Robert Kirkman, ed. "Style to Which They Were Accustomed." *The Matrimonial Strategist* (January 1991).

Czapanskiy, Karen. "Volunteers and Draftees: The Struggle for Parental Equality." *UCLA Law Review* (1991).

Dobris, Joel C. "Medicaid Asset Planning by the Elderly: A Policy View of Expectations, Entitlement and Inheritance." *Real Property, Probate, and Trust Journal* (Spring 1989).

Dodson, Diane. "A Guide to the Guidelines." *Family Advocate* (Spring 1988).

Freed, Doris Jonas, and Timothy B. Walker, eds. "Family Law in the Fifty States: An Overview." *Family Law Quarterly* (Winter 1991).

Garneau, George. "Newhouse Wins Tax Case." *Editor and Publisher* (March 10, 1990).

Johnson, Elizabeth Richie. "I Couldn't Afford My Job." *Redbook* (April 21, 1991).

Kagan, Julia, and Rosalind C. Barnett. "Money Mastery." *Working Woman* (December 1986).

Lerner, Ralph E. "Putting a Price on Art." *The National Law Journal* (June 17, 1991).

Lewin, Tamar. "For Some Two-Paycheck Families, the Economics Don't Add Up." *The New York Times* (April 21, 1991).

Morris, Michele, and Alexandria Siegel. "The Thirteenth Annual *Working Woman* Salary Survey 1992." *Working Woman* (January 1992).

Otten, Alan L. "Farm Belt Holds Onto Its Oldest Americans." *Wall Street Journal* (September 4, 1991).

Paulson, C. Morton. "What If You Couldn't Work Anymore?" *Changing Times* (August, 1990).

Potuchek, Jean L. "Who's Responsible for Supporting the Family? Employed Wives and the Breadwinner Role." Working Paper No. 186, Wellesley College, Center for Research on Women, 1988.

Schafran, Lynn Hecht. "Gender Bias in the Courts: An Emerging Focus for Judicial Reform." *Arizona State Law Journal* 21 (1989).

Schoen, Robert, William Urton, Karen Woodrow, and John Baj. "Marriage and Divorce in Twentieth Century American Cohorts." *Demography* (February 1985).

Schultz, Ellen C. "When It's the Wrong Time for Big Financial Decisions." *Wall Street Journal* (October 29, 1991).

Schultz, Marjorie Maguire. "Contractual Ordering of Marriage: A New Model for State Policy." *California Law Review* (March 1982).

Seneker, Harold, ed., with Dolores Lataniotis. "The Richest People in America." *Forbes* (October 21, 1991).

Shelton, Beth Ann. "The Distribution of Household Tasks: Does Wife's Employment Make a Difference?" *Journal of Family Issues* (June 1990).

Sherman, Rorie. "Billed for Sex?" *National Law Journal* (August 1991).

Sheppard, Annamay T. "Women, Families and Equality: Was Divorce Reform a Mistake?" *Women's Rights Law Reporter* (Fall 1990).

Somerset, Lady Anne. "Elizabeth I." *Connoisseur* (November 1991).

Stanley, Sandra C., Janet G. Hunt, and Larry L. Hunt. "The Relative Deprivation of Husbands in Dual-Earner Households." *Journal of Family Issues* (March 1986).

Tobias, Carl. "Interspousal Tort Immunity in America." *Georgia Law Review* 23 (1989).

Topolnicki, Denise M. "How to Get What's Coming to You." *Savvy* (November 1989).

Vikan, Gary. "Art and Marriage in Early Christianity." *The Walters Art Gallery Monthly Bulletin* (October 1991).

Voydanoff, Patricia. "Economic Distress and Family Relations: A Review of the Eighties." *Journal of Marriage and the Family* (November 1990).

Waldman, Steven. "Deadbeat Dads." *Newsweek* (May 4, 1992).

Walker, Timothy B. "Family Law in the Fifty States: An Overview." *Family Law Quarterly* (Winter 1992).

Wardle, Lynn D. "No-Fault Divorce and the Divorce Conundrum." *Brigham Young University Law Review* (1991).

Wenig, Mary Moers. "The Marital Property Law of Connecticut: Past, Present and Future." *Wisconsin Law Review* 3 (1990).

White, Lynn K., and Shenming Tang. "The Economic Foundations of Marital Happiness and Divorce." Paper presented at the 1991 meetings of Midwest Sociological Society, Des Moines, Iowa, March 1992.

Weisbert, Lynn. "A Marriage Made . . . by Satellite?" *National Law Journal* (March 4, 1991).

Younger, Judith T. "Perspectives on Antenuptial Agreements." *Rutgers Law Review* 40 (1988).

Wiener, Victor. "Recent Cases Highlight Complications Involved in Selecting an Appraiser." *The National Law Journal* (June 17, 1991).

Additional Readings

Marriage

American Bar Association, Public Education Division. *Your Legal Guide to Marriage.* Chicago: American Bar Association, 1983.

Felton-Collins, Victoria. *Couples & Money: Why Money Interferes with Love & What to Do About It.* New York: Bantam Books, 1990.

Sager, Clifford, and Bernice Hunt. *Intimate Partners: Hidden Patterns in Love Relationships.* New York: McGraw-Hill, 1979.

Warner, Ralph, Toni Ihara, and Stephen Elias. *California Marriage & Divorce Law.* Berkeley, Calif.: Nolo Press, 1990.

Divorce

Briles, Judith. *The Dollars and Sense of Divorce: The Financial Guide for Women.* New York: Master Media Limited, 1988.

De Angelis, Sidney M. *You're Entitled!: A Divorce Lawyer Talks to Women.* Chicago: Contemporary Books, Inc. 1989.

Engel, Margorie L., and Diana D. Gould. *The Divorce Decisions Workbook: A Planning and Action Guide.* New York: McGraw-Hill, 1992.

Friedman, James T. *The Divorce Handbook: Your Basic Guide to Divorce Updated.* New York: Random House, 1982.

Harwood, Norma. *A Woman's Legal Guide to Separation and Divorce in All 50 States.* New York: Charles Scribner's Sons, 1985.

Jacob, Herbert. *Silent Revolution: The Transformation of Divorce Law in the United States.* Chicago: University of Chicago Press, 1988.

Lake, Steven R. *Rematch: Winning Legal Battles with Your Ex.* Chicago: Chicago Review Press, 1989.

McConaughey, Dan E. *Georgia: Divorce, Alimony and Child Custody.* Norcross, Ga.: The Harrison Company, 1990.

Robertson, Christina. *A Woman's Guide to Divorce and Decision Making.* New York: Simon and Schuster, 1988.

Samuelson, Elliot D. *The Divorce Law Handbook: A Comprehensive Guide to Matrimonial Practice.* New York: Insight Books, 1988.

Stone, Lawrence. *Road to Divorce: England 1530–1987.* New York: Oxford University Press, 1992.

Woodhouse, Violet, Victoria Felton-Collins, and M. C. Blakeman. *Divorce & Money: Everything You Need to Know About Dividing Property.* Berkeley, Calif.: Nolo Press, 1992.

Retirement and Estate Planning

American Association of Retired Persons. *How to Plan Your Successful Retirement.* San Francisco: ACCESS Press/The Understanding Business, 1988.

American Bar Association, Section of General Practice. *All-States Wills and Estate Planning Guide.* Chicago: American Bar Association, 1990.

Appel, Jens C., and F. Bruce Gentry. *The Complete Will Kit.* New York: John Wiley & Sons, 1990.

Lester, Toni P. *How to Settle an Estate or Prepare Your Will.* New York: Perigee Books, 1988.

Patterson, Martha Priddy. *The Working Woman's Guide to Retirement Planning.* Englewood Cliffs, N.J.: Prentice Hall, 1993.

Quinn, Jane Bryant. *Making the Most of Your Money.* New York: Simon and Schuster, 1991.

Money Management

Card, Emily. *The Ms. Money Book: Strategies for Prospering in the Coming Decade.* New York: E.P. Dutton, 1990.
Leonard, Robin. *Money Troubles: Legal Strategies to Cope with Your Debts.* Berkeley, Calif.: Nolo Press, 1991.

Status and History of Women

Aries, Philippe, and Georges Duby, eds. *A History of Private Life from Pagan Rome to Byzantium,* Vol. I. Cambridge, Mass.: The Belknap Press of Harvard University Press, 1987.
Fuchs, Victor R. *Women's Quest for Economic Equality.* Cambridge, Mass.: Havard University Press, 1988.
Leonard, Frances. *Women and Money: The Independent Woman's Guide to Financial Security for Life.* New York: Addison-Wesley Publishing Company, Inc., 1991.
Mason, Mary Ann. *The Equality Trap.* New York: Simon and Schuster, 1988.

Acknowledgments

Thanks to so many.

Writing a book about marriage and money means you are writing a book to which just about everyone will have something to add—some little anecdote, some personal experience that helped enrich my perspective. Throughout the book, I refer to many of my friends who were willing to entrust their stories to me. I have changed their names and their situations to ensure their privacy. But I thank them all for their help.

Many others helped me as well. Geraldine Fabrikant of *The New York Times* gets my first thanks, for she knew I had an outline for a book stuck away in a drawer and encouraged me to meet Ed Victor, who became my agent. Ed Victor's belief, from the start, that my one-page outline could become a book was the catalyst I needed. Joni Evans, my editor, publisher, and friend, never failed to steer me in the right direction. She patiently coped with my anxieties, and was always there when I needed her.

Much of the work on this book was done at the Writer's Room in New York, a sanctuary that provided the atmosphere I needed in order to complete my work.

I was also fortunate in being able to call upon many of the outstanding practitioners in the fields of law, insurance, money management, marital counseling, and financial planning. I would like to thank especially Robert Wittes, who patiently read many chapters, as well as William Zabel, Robert Cohen, Connie Chen, and Peter Roth.

Alan Wachtel shared his insights gleaned from many years of family therapy practice. Gary Strum cheerfully crunched many numbers for me. The late Ernest Sommer was a guide through the financial world. Neal Rifkin and Ken Weisberg continued the tradition.

Especially helpful whenever I called were the various experts at the Bureau of the Census who were willing to supply any number of statistics that are cited in the notes.

Natasha Gray, who toiled as research assistant, gets special mention for all her efforts.

Then there were the many who were willing to answer my questions, strangers who were kind enough to take time from their own busy schedules to find a reference, send me an article, or otherwise give me information.

Linda Barbanel, Dr. Clifford Sager, and Violet Woodhouse answered many questions about money and marriage. Stanley L. Goodman gave a straightforward account of the problems of evaluation. Eleanor Alter, Harriet Newman Cohen, Thomas M. Mulroy, and Barry Meadows were all experts on the problems of women and divorce. Peter Strauss and Yisroel Schulman were guides to the world of elder-care law. Family Planners Janet Kovanda, Maxine Hyrkas, Claire S. Langden, Mary McGrath, and Margaret Tracy were among those who provided great help.

Vincent Gandolfo, William Lockwood, Lenard Marlow, Glen Henkel, Mary Moers Wenig, Alexander Folger, Marvin Snyder, Stanley Lipton, Deborah Batts, and Robert George all contributed, and The Stuart Planning Seminar kindly allowed me to attend a seminar.

The Turtle Bay Books staff were all always a pleasure to work with, and particular thanks to my copy editor, Gail Bradney.

Index

Index

fault in, 100
grounds for, 68, 69–72
history of, 68–69
houses and, 93, 227
housewife's contribution and,
76–77, 98, 99
lawyers for, see Divorce lawyers
legal clinics for, 102
mediators in, 102–5
negotiation in, 107–8
no-fault, 69–72, 87
and prenuptial agreements, 52
preparations for, 95–101
property settlements in, 72–80,
117–18, 228
reforms, 87–94
residency requirements for, 71–72
routes to, 102–5
Social Security and, 122
and standard of living, 79–80, 98,
99
taxes and, 93, 226–28
temporary support in, 106–8
valuing pensions for, 214–17
when to settle in, 115–16
wills in, 175
women losing in, 94–95
and working women, 9
Divorce lawyers
and chances for success, 112–15
and costs, 110–12
questions before hiring, 108–10
Dower rights, 20
Durable powers of attorney, 153

Earnings, future, 77–78, 84
Elective shares, 165
Employers, and pension plans, 123,
136–37
Equitable distribution, 73–77, 89,
93
Equitable reimbursement, 79
ESOPs, 125
Estate freezes, 186
Estate planning, 172–73
Estates
defined, 183

dower and curtesy rights in, 20
executors of, 166, 177, 183–84
and taxes, 164, 166, 170–73, 183,
194, 230–31
valuation of property in, 213–20
Executors, 166, 177, 183–84
Expenses
calculation of, 36–37
guidelines for, 39–40
sharing of, 42–43, 46, 47

Families
as corporations, 32–33
as interested third parties, 55–56
power in, 15–16
Fault, in divorce, 100
Felder, Raoul, 150–51
Ferraro, Geraldine, 13
FICA, see Social Security
Financial disclosure, 60
Financial planners, 144–49
Fonda, Jane, 95
Forced shares, 165
Forward averaging tax breaks,
229
401(k) and 403(b) pension plans,
124–25, 127, 128
Funerals, planning for, 189–90

Gastineau, Mark, 100
Gerard, Jean and James, 170
Getty, J. Paul, 167
Gifts
of stocks, 186
and taxes, 173
Goldman, Sandra and Peter, 79–80,
88
Golub, Richard, 77–78
Graham, Katharine, 174

Hidden assets, hunt for, 101–2,
223–26
Houses
in community property states, 24,
25
divorce and, 93, 227
sale of, 194–96, 227, 229–30

Index

ABOUT THE TYPE

This book was set in Electra, a typeface designed for Linotype
by W. A. Dwiggins, the renowned type designer (1880–1956).
Electra is a fluid typeface, avoiding the contrasts of thick and
thin strokes that are prevalent in most modern typefaces.